The Rights of Gun Owners

Other books by Alan M. Gottlieb:

The Gun Owners Political Action Manual
The Gun Grabbers
Gun Rights Fact Book
Wise Use Agenda

A Second Amendment
Foundation Handbook

THE
RIGHTS OF
GUN OWNERS

ALAN GOTTLIEB

Merril Press
Bellevue, Washington

Acknowledgments

I wish to express my tremendous gratitude to the brilliant research director of the Second Amendment Foundation, Talcott J. Franklin, who worked closely with me on this project; to John Barnett, the projects director of the Second Amendment Foundation, for his help and guidance with the chapter on the constitutional rights of gun ownership and to John Hosford, executive director of the Citizens Committee for the Right to Keep and Bear Arms, for his help and direction with the chapter dealing with the basic issues of gun control; and to Susan Elings, my secretary for all the long hard hours of keyboarding all the information contained in this book. Of course, this book would never have been written if it were not for the hundreds of thousands of individuals who have contributed to the Second Amendment Foundation's outstanding programs and projects.

All inquiries and catalog request should be addressed to Merril Press, P.O. Box 1682, Bellevue WA, 98009.

Library of Congress cataloging-in-Publication Data
Gottlieb, Alan M.
  The rights of gun owners : a Second Amendment Foundation handbook / Alan Gottlieb.
        p.   cm.
  Includes bibliographical references.
  ISBN 0-936783-07-9 : $9.95
  1. Firearms--Law and registration--United States--Miscellanea.
  2. Firearms--Law and legistion--United States--States. I. Second Amendment Foundation. II. Title.
  KF3941.Z9G675 1991
  344.73'0533--dc20
  [347.304533]   91-31859
                                                       CIP

Acknowledgments

I wish to express my tremendous gratitude to the brilliant research director of the Second Amendment Foundation, Talcott J. Franklin, who worked closely with me on this project; to John Barnett, the projects director of the Second Amendment Foundation, for his help and guidance with the chapter on the constitutional rights of gun ownership and to John Hosford, executive director of the Citizens Committee for the Right to Keep and Bear Arms, for his help and direction with the chapter dealing with the basic issues of gun control; and to Susan Elings, my secretary for all the long hard hours of keyboarding all the information contained in this book. Of course, this book would never have been written if it were not for the hundreds of thousands of individuals who have contributed to the Second Amendment Foundation's outstanding programs and projects.

All inquiries and catalog request should be addressed to Merril Press, P.O. Box 1682, Bellevue WA, 98009

To

Julie, my dear wife, who has shared much hard work and many long hours, and without whose help, nothing anymore would be possible.

And to

Those gun owners who have suffered at the hands of the Bureau of Alcohol, Tobacco and Firearms (BATF), as well as from other government bureaucratic and regulatory agencies, who make this book necessary.

One need only look at Ken Ballew, David Moorhead, and the thousands of other honorable American gun owners who have been unjustly victimized by BATF, which callously engages in unconscionable entrapment practices against the lawful gun-owning public.

I hope this book will help educate America's gun owners as to what their rights are, how those rights are being destroyed, and how to protect themselves from a government grown too powerful.

Contents

Introduction

by Congressman Philip Crane

I am pleased to recommend this book to those concerned about the erosion of our Second Amendment rights. Current political dialogue is rife with talk of the rights of this or that group — women, minorities, prisoners, and the like. Regrettably, there is no serious discussion, either in government or the media, of the constitutional and statutory rights of America's 100 million gun owners. Alan Gottlieb's book fills this void in a very informative way.

In my ten years in Congress I've witnessed the decline of one aspect of the anti-gun movement, and the use of a more insidious form of gun control.

The passage of the Gun Control Act of 1968 ('68 GCA) marked the political apex of the anti-gun movement. Since then the political power and public support of gun prohibitionists have waned. That no major piece of federal legislation regulating handguns has been enacted since the '68 GCA attests the decline. In liberal Massachusetts, in 1976, a measure to ban handguns was defeated by a landslide 2 to 1 margin.

The passage of legislation sponsored by Senator James McClure (R-Idaho) to repeal some of the more repressive provisions of the '68 GCA is further evidence of the gun prohibitionists' decline.

Having been thus thwarted in the legislative arena, gun prohibitionists are turning increasingly to local government and the federal bureaucracy as vehicles for disarmament. In light of urban attitudes toward the misuse of handguns, big-city mayors and police bureaucrats are among the most ardent supporters of gun control. The U.S. Conference of Mayors, through its handgun control staff, has been in the forefront of those advocating the confiscation of privately owned arms.

In August, 1979, Evanston, Illinois, passed an ordinance prohibiting the sale of firearms and ammunition in the town limits. A few months later New Haven, Connecticut, adopted a similar measure.

Licenses to possess or carry a handgun, which are required in most states, are usually issued by local police. In recent years some police departments have adopted an increasingly arbitrary policy on issuing the licenses — often requiring applicants to prove that they have a special need to possess a handgun. Such local policies frequently contravene that state's constitutional right to keep and bear arms clause or licensing statute.

The Bureau of Alcohol, Tobacco and Firearms, an agency of the Department of Treasury, is charged with enforcing federal firearms laws. It is responsible for licensing and regulating the nation's gun dealers. Since the bureau's activities in the areas of alcohol and tobacco have declined in recent years, BATF has expanded its anti-gun operations.

Congressional hearings have thoroughly documented BATF's violations of civil liberties, violations which have become standard operating procedure for the bureau. Through questionable activities, including various forms of harassment, BATF has sought to increase its prosecution of gun owners, and thereby enhance its image. Also, at various times, the agency has put forth thinly disguised plans for the national registration of handguns. The following are a few of the many instances of BATF activism in regulating the firearms trade:

* In 1971, BATF agents and local deputy sheriffs broke into the Silver Spring, Maryland, apartment of gun collector Ken Ballew and shot him in the head. The agents said they were looking for unregistered handguns and grenades. None was found, although a U.S. district court judge later ruled that Ballew possessed the components to manufacture grenades. As a result of the bureau's inap-

propriate enforcement of 1968 Gun Control Act, Ballew is partially paralyzed for life.

* In 1978 BATF agents and officers of the Santa Clara sheriff's office raided the San Jose Gun Show. For three hours they detained some three hundred and fifty patrons and exhibitors. The "purpose" of the raid was to distribute information on alleged violations of federal firearms law that occur at gun show. Many of the dealers were interrogated and patrons were photographed and otherwise harassed.

* On October 22, 1978, Elmer Turngren was sleeping and his wife reading religious material when some thirty local policemen and BATF agents raided their house in Kirkland, Washington. Acting on information from an unidentified informant, the bureau searched for illegal explosives, machine-guns, and drugs. No contraband was discovered. The family was forced to stand in the cold while the agents, toting automatic weapons, vainly ransacked their home.

* James Kehrer has operated a gun shop in Niles, Michigan, for the past twenty-one years. In October 1979 he was informed that his federal firearms license, which every dealer must have to do business, would not be renewed. BATF's reason for putting Kehrer out of business was that he failed to maintain proper sales records. The casual observer might attribute this to the fact that bureau agents had seized his records and kept them for one and a half years in an attempt to uncover some infraction of the law. Unsuccessful in that endeavor, BATF proceeded to create a circumstance in which Kehrer could be held in violation of another of the bureau's standards.

To defend their rights from increasing incursions by bureaucrats at all levels of government, gun owners must know exactly what those rights are, as well as their historic derivation. For those concerned about the preservation and extension of freedom of gun ownership, this book is an excellent primer.

Chapter 1

Constitutional History of the Individual Right to Keep and Bear Arms

WHAT IS THE SECOND AMENDMENT?

The Second Amendment to the United States Constitution, passed by Congress on September 25, 1789, and ratified by three-fourths of the states on December 15, 1791, states: "A well regulated Militia, being necessary to the security of a free State, the right of the people to keep and bear Arms, shall not be infringed."

It is important to note that this guarantee of the right to keep and bear arms was considered so important that it was preceded only by freedom of speech, press, and religion in the Bill of Rights. In fact, when ratification of the Constitution was being considered in the state legislatures, many states refused to approve the Constitution unless the federal government should promise to add an amendment on freedom of gun ownership at the earliest opportunity.

Why was the Second Amendment included in the Bill of Rights?

The Founding Fathers had an abiding fear of government. At the time the Constitution was drafted they had just concluded a long and bloody war against one form of tyranny. However, they were equally concerned about the kind of government they had just established.

Their concern was that a centralized federal government

1

could evolve into a dictatorship. They viewed the federal armed forces, which the Constitution authorized, as a potential vehicle for suppressing dissent. In the words of Samuel Adams, "A standing army, however necessary it may be at some times, is always dangerous to the liberties of the people. Such power should be watched with a jealous eye." [1]

The framers of the Constitution believed that a well-armed populace would serve as an effective counterbalance to a standing army and as a bulwark of liberty. In the Federalist Papers Alexander Hamilton tried to counter the prevalent fear of a standing army by asserting that liberty would always be ensured, as long as the people were allowed to be "properly armed and equipped."[2] Also in the Federalist Papers James Madison, author of the Second Amendment, writes that even under the Constitution (with its federal army) "the ultimate authority...resides in the people alone [under our Constitution, due to] the advantage of being armed which the Americans possess over the people of almost every other nation."[3]

Perhaps the sentiments of our colonial forebears are best summarized by Joseph Story, an associate justice of the United States Supreme Court (1812-45) and one of our foremost constitutional scholars. In his magnum opus, Three Commentaries on the Constitution of the United States (1833), Story wrote: "The right of the citizens to keep and bear arms has justly been considered the palladium of the liberties of the republic; since it offers a strong moral check against the usurpation and arbitrary powers of rulers; and will generally, even if these are successful in the first instance, enable the people to resist and triumph over them."

How did the Founding Fathers feel about the right to keep and bear arms?

The Founding Fathers were mindful of the important role civilian gun ownership played in the American Revolution. In the Declaration of Causes and Necessity of Taking up Arms (July 6, 1775), one of the causes cited for the rebellion was that the British seized the arms of the inhabitants of Boston. Indeed, the famous "shot heard round the world" (the battles of Lexington and Concord) was precipitated by the Red Coats' attempt to confiscate the Minutemen's store of arms.

With this experience fresh in his memory, Thomas Jefferson provided in his Virginia Constitution of 1776 that "no free man shall be debarred the use of arms within his own land."

Said Patrick Henry: "The great object is that every man be armed—everyone who is able may have a gun."[4] George Washington, commander of the Continental army, was particularly appreciative of the importance of firearms in the struggle for freedom. Said he, "A free people ought ... to be armed."[5] Thomas Paine, one of the greatest philosophers of the time, argued, "The supposed quietude of a good man allures the ruffian; while on the other hand, arms like laws discourage and keep the invader and plunderer in awe, and preserve order in the world as well as property."[6]

In fact, the colonial leaders were so enamored of weapons that one might almost call them "gun nuts." In a letter of advice to his nephew, Jefferson praises the gun in developing a keen mind. "A strong body makes the mind strong. As to the species of exercises, I advise the gun. While this gives moderate exercise to the body, it gives boldness, enterprise and independence to the mind."[7]

Naturally the colonials were anxious to guarantee what they believed one of the foremost freedoms. In the Massachusetts convention, Sam Adams, that old revolutionary firebrand, introduced the resolution that the "Constitution shall never be construed to authorize Congress to prevent the people of the United States who are peaceable citizens from keeping their own arms."[8]

What are the common-law origins of the Second Amendment?

Sir William Blackstone (1725-80), considered the definitive chronicler of English common law, had this to say of the right to keep and bear arms in his commentaries (on the common law): "Of the absolute rights of individuals: the fifth and last auxiliary right of the subject...is that of having arms for their defense." He went on to explain that the basis for this right is the "natural right of resistance and self-preservation when the sanctions of society and laws are found insufficient to restrain the violence of oppression."

By the time Blackstone wrote his Commentaries there was a well-established right to keep and bear arms both for self-protection and for defense of the realm The English Bill of Rights of 1689 provided that "the subjects which are Protestants, may have arms for their defense suitable to their condition and as allowed by law."

This right to arms can be traced back to the Anglo-Saxon military establishment of Alfred the Great (C.E. 870), known as the fyrd. The fyrd consisted of three divisions: the king's troops (or house guard)--a very small force; the select fyrd--civilians who drilled at regular intervals and were paid out of the treasury while on duty; and the general fyrd--composed of every able-bodied male citizen of the kingdom, who was required to arm himself at his own expense.

This tradition of imposing a legal duty on citizens to keep arms in defense of the nation was carried forward with the Assize of Arms of Henry II (1181) and the Statute of Winchester, of Edward I. The Statute of Northampton (Edward III), which provided that "none may go armed to the terror of the populace," is often cited by antigunners. However, the ordinance really referred to bearing arms in a threatening or intimidating way, so as to terrorize the populace.

Henry VIII in 1511 required all British citizens, under the age of forty, to possess and train with a long bow--the deadliest weapon of the time. His daughter Mary Tudor required the citizen militia to have firearms. One of the principal complaints against James II (who was overthrown in the Glorious Revolution) and enunciated in the aforementioned Bill of Rights, was "causing several good subjects which are Protestants to be disarmed."

In the eight hundred years from Alfred the Great's general fyrd to the Glorious Revolution there developed the concept of the male populace keeping and bearing arms as a line of national defense. This was reinforced by many statutes and proclamations.

What "militia" in the Second Amendment means.

People argue interminably about the meaning of "militia" in the Second Amendment. But there's really no need for this confusion. One need only look at the writings and speeches of the Founding Fathers to determine what the drafters of the Constitution, and their contemporaries, meant.

In debating the ratification of the Constitution before the Virginia Assembly (June 16, 1788), George Mason stated, "I ask who are the militia? They consist now of the whole people, except a few public officials."[9] Patrick Henry concurred. In 1811 Thomas Jefferson elucidated the subject thus, in a letter to a friend: "The true barriers of our liberty in this country are our state governments." He maintained that a potential federal dictatorship would always be opposed by state militias, made up of "every man able to bear arms."[10]

In fact, drafters of the Militia Act of 1792, enacted shortly after the adoption of the Constitution, studied the Swiss model, which is just such a citizen militia, and sent to Switzerland for documents on its operation.

It is quite clear that by "militia" the founders meant every able-bodied man.

Has militia ever been defined by statute or otherwise?

Indeed it has. Webster's dictionary defines militia as, "1. a part of the organized armed forces of a country liable to call only in emergency. 2. the whole body of able-bodied male citizens declared by law as being subject to call for military service" (*Webster's New Collegiate Dictionary* [1988], p. 753). A different version of *Webster's* is even more specific: "2. in the United States, all able-bodied male citizens between 18 and 45 years old who are not already members of the regular armed forces: members of the National Guard, Organized Reserve Corps, and the Naval and Marine Reserves constitute the organized militia; all others, the unorganized militia."[11]

The statutory definition of militia has remained relatively unchanged, from the first Militia Act (1792) to the present. On January 21, 1903, Congress defined the militia as consisting of all able-bodied male citizens "more than 18 and less than 45 years of age."

USC 1970 Title 10 (311 Militia: Composition and Classes--states, "The militia of the United States consists of all able-bodied males at least 17 years of age and, except as provided in section 313 of title 32, under 45 years of age who are, or who have made declaration of intention to become, citizens of the United States and of female citizens of the United States who are commissioned officers of the National Guard.

"The classes of the militia are--

"(1) the organized militia, which consists of the National Guard and the Naval Militia; and

"(2) the unorganized militia, which consists of the members of the militia who are not members of the National Guard or Naval Militia."

Gun-control advocates say the Second Amendment applies only to state militias, i.e., the National Guard. Is this true?

Most certainly not. Again, the colonial leaders were quite specific about what they meant by the term "militia." During debates on the ratification of the Constitution, New Hampshire proposed this amendment: "Congress shall never disarm any citizens unless such as are or have been in Actual Rebellion."[12] An amendment sponsored by Pennsylvania (1787) stated that "the people have a right to bear arms for the defense of themselves or their own state or the United States."[13]

Perhaps the foremost authority on the meaning of the Second Amendment is the author of the amendment, James Madison. In *The Federalist Papers,* number 46, Madison tells readers not to worry about usurpation of authority by a federal army, which will, if necessary, be opposed by "a militia amounting to near half a million men."[14] Since the free adult male population was only about 800,000 in 1790, it is safe to assume that Madison wasn't referring to state reserves in this article. By militia, Madison meant every able-bodied man, capable of bearing arms in defense of himself and the state, and it is in this sense that he used the term in the Second Amendment. Jefferson employed the same concept of militia when he stated, "We cannot be defended but by making every citizen a soldier."

In a floor debate on the Bill of Rights in the United States Senate, a motion to add the words "for the common defense" after the words "to keep and bear arms" was soundly defeated.

The antigun forces have (perhaps deliberately) confused militia with the semimilitary groups, such as the Minutemen, known as "trained bands" (or select militia). These later forces evolved into the state militias and eventually the National Guard. However, that was not what Madison and the other leaders of the newly founded Republic meant by militia. Richard Henry Lee, a signer of the Declaration of Independence, not only was opposed to a federal army, but was equally adverse to a select militia, which he felt was also a potential threat to freedom. It is clear from the entire common law history of the right to keep and bear arms that this was a right conferred on the general militia (the people at large), not the select militia.

Last, it is important to keep in mind that the Second Amendment confers two separate rights--the right to keep arms and the right to bear arms. If the right to bear arms was only a right conferred on state reserves, why couple it with the right to keep arms? State reserves only need arms while in the field. Their weapons are stored at armories. Only the general militia, the people themselves, need the right to keep arms as well.

To whom does the "people" refer in the Second Amendment?

Again the antigunners have attempted to distort the meaning of the Second Amendment. They assert that the "people" guaranteed this right is the nation as a whole (or the government), not individuals. This flies in the face of court decisions and constitutional scholarship. The First Amendment's "right of the people to assemble peaceably and petition the government for a redress of grievances" has been interpreted by the Supreme Court as an individual right. Similarly, the Fourth Amendment guarantee of "the right of the people to be secure in their persons, houses, papers, and effects, against unreasonable searches and seizures" has been interpreted as pertaining to individuals. If the term "people" means individuals everywhere else in the Bill of Rights, why should we suppose that it has an entirely different meaning in the Second Amendment?

A recent Supreme Court decision leaves little doubt as to the meaning of the term "the people" used in the Second Amendment. In *US v. Verdugo-Urquidez*, the Court held that "the people" referred to "a class of persons who are part of a national community..."

"... 'the people' seems to have been a term of art employed in select parts of the Constitution," wrote the Court. "The Preamble declares that the Constitution is ordained and established by 'the people of the United States.' The Second Amendment protects 'the right of the people to keep and bear Arms,' and the Ninth and Tenth Amendments provide that certain rights and powers are retained by and reserved to 'the people.'"

Let us again consider the writings of the author of the Second Amendment. In *The Federalist Papers,* Madison states that "the governments [of Europe] are afraid to trust the people with arms."[15] We can assume Madison was referring to individuals because he contrasted "people" to government, which refused to recognize the people's right to be armed.

The Second Amendment speaks of a "well-regulated" militia being necessary to the security of a free state. Does this modify the right to keep and bear arms?

The term "well regulated" is an expression of one objective to be achieved by the exercise of the right, not a limitation on the right to keep and bear arms. It is not that the right is limited to the purpose of well regulating the militia. Rather, it was the hope of the Founding Fathers that the exercise of this right would lead to the existence of a well-regulated militia. As Second Amendment scholar Dr. David Caplan puts it, "The right to keep and bear arms serves to well-regulate the militia; rather than have the militia being well regulated [controlled] by a government whose leadership is bent on tyranny."[16]

Attorney David Hardy, writing in *Restricting Handguns: The Liberal Skeptics Speak Out,* concurs with that assessment: "It [the collective rights argument] renders this term meaningless, since it is obvious that prohibiting federal disarmament of militia units does not ensure that they will be well regulated, as armament and organization have at best a most tangential relationship. A guarantee against disarmament may ensure the existence of an armed militia, but not a well-regulated one."[17]

Only by interpreting the Second Amendment as an individual right does the term "well regulated" make sense. If individuals have a right to keep and bear arms, which they exercise, that will well-regulate the militia.

Has the Supreme Court ruled on the meaning of the Second Amendment?

There have been only three Supreme Court cases directly on the Second Amendment, two of them in the nineteenth century. In *U.S. v.. Cruikshank,* 92 U.S. 542 (1876), and *Presser v. Illinois,* 116 U.S. 252 (1886), the Court held that the Second Amendment doesn't apply to the states. During that era the Supreme Court also held that the First Amendment freedoms of speech, press, and religion, the Fourth Amendment protection from unreasonable search and seizure, and the Fifth Amendment freedom from self-incrimination also did not apply to the states. However, in the twentieth century the Court has ruled that all of these rights are incorporated into the Fourteenth Amendment, and thus applicable to the states.

The most recent Supreme Court case was decided almost

fifty years ago. In *United States v. Miller,* 307 U.S. 174 (1939), the Court ruled on the constitutionality of the National Firearms Act of 1936, as it applied to a ban on the interstate transport of sawed-off shotguns. The decision specified, "The Court cannot take judicial notice that a shotgun having a barrel less than 18 inches long has today any reasonable relation to the preservation or efficiency of a well-regulated militia; and therefore cannot say that the Second Amendment guarantees to the citizen the right to keep and bear such a weapon."

It is important to bear in mind that the Court did not define "militia." If, as we believe, the militia comprises the whole people, then under this interpretation of the Second Amendment we have the constitutional right to keep and bear any arms related to the maintenance of the militia. A more recent Supreme Court case, *Lewis v. U.S.,* 63 L Ed 2d 198 U.S. Supreme Court Reports (1980), touches briefly on the Second Amendment, but only to repeat the weapons-as-related-to-militia therory of the Miller Court.

Has the Supreme Court ever changed its mind about the meaning of various sections of the Constitution?

The history of Supreme Court decisions is one of constant change and reinterpretation of the Constitution. *United States v. Miller* is not written in stone. It is quite likely that a future Supreme Court, or even the current Court, will interpret the Second Amendment differently. Here are just a few examples of instances in which the Court has completely reversed its interpretation of the Constitution:

In *Plessy v. Ferguson* (1896) the Court upheld the constitutionality of racial segregation (separate but equal facilities). It held that the Fourteenth Amendment was a guarantee of political, not social, equality. A little more than fifty years later the Court reversed itself in *Brown v. Board of Education of Topeka* (1954), holding that segregation violated the equal-protection clause of the Fourteenth Amendment.

The Court defined obscenity in *Roth v. United States* (1957) as "utterly without redeeming social value" and declared that such material is not protected by the First Amendment. In 1973, *Miller v. California,* the Court rejected the "utterly without redeeming social value" test of the *Roth* decision and substituted community standards for determining obscenity.

In *Ohmstead v. United States* (1928) the Court held that wiretapping is not an unconstitutional search or seizure. In *Katz v. U.S.* (1967) the Court held it was.

In *Twining v. New Jersey* (1908) the Court ruled that the exemption of self-incrimination of the Fifth Amendment was not applicable to the states. This was overruled in *Malloy v. Hogan* (1964).

Palko v. Connecticut (1937) held that the Fifth Amendment guarantee of double jeopardy was not applicable to the states. This was overruled in *Benton v. Maryland* (1969).

What weapons does the Second Amendment guarantee cover?

As Supreme Court Justice Hugo Black stated in 1975, "Although the Supreme Court has held this amendment to include only arms necessary to a well-regulated militia, as so construed, its prohibition is absolute." In other words, under *U.S. v. Miller* any arms related to the maintenance of the militia are covered by the constitutional protection.

At the very least this should include handguns (which are often used as military side arms) and long arms (rifles and shotguns).

Do the states have right-to-keep-and-bear-arms clauses in their constitutions?

Indeed they do. Forty-three states have such constitutional guarantees. Many are much stronger (more specific) than the Second Amendment.

For instance, twenty-two states frame this guarantee expressly as an individual right, speaking in such terms as the defense of person, property, home, and the like.

Here are a few examples of very strong state constitutional

provisions:

Alabama- "That every citizen has a right to bear arms in defense of himself and the state" (Article 1, Section 26).

Arizona- "The right of the individual to bear arms in defense of himself or the state shall not be impaired." (Article 2, Section 26).

Kansas- "The people have the right to bear arms for their defense and security..." (Article 1, Section 4).

Montana- "The right of any person to keep or bear arms in defense of his home, person, or property ... shall not be called in question..." (Article 2, Section 12).

New Mexico- "No law shall abridge the right of the citizen to keep and bear arms for security and defense, for hunting and recreational use, and for other lawful purposes..." (Article 2, Section 6).

If you challenge a law as an abridgment of your right to keep and bear arms, it will probably be a state statute or local ordinance. Therefore, you should check your state constitution first, to see if it gives you support in your legal efforts. Chances are it will.

Are any other sections of the Constitution relevant to freedom of gun ownership?

Most gun owners naturally think of the Second Amendment, when they consider constitutional protection of the right to keep and bear arms. However, there are several constitutional amendments that offer additional support for gun owners.

The Ninth Amendment provides, "The enumeration in the Constitution of certain rights shall not be construed to deny or disparage others retained by the people." In other words, because certain traditional common-law rights, such as the right to armed self-defense, aren't spelled out specifically in the Constitution, it doesn't mean that these rights have been nullified.

The Fourth Amendment protects Americans from unreasonable search and seizure. This constitutional guarantee is routinely violated by the police in making arrests for unlawful possession of a firearm or carrying a concealed weapon. Violations may occur in the search of a dwelling, automobile, or individual (patdown).

The Fourteenth Amendment provides, in part, "No state shall make or enforce any law which shall abridge the privileges or immunities of citizens of the United States; nor shall any state deprive any person of life, liberty, or property, without due process of law; nor deny to any person within its jurisdiction the equal protection of the law."

That amendment passed Congress in 1866, shortly after the conclusion of the Civil War. It was aimed at states of the former Confederacy, which were routinely abridging the rights of newly freed blacks. In fact, some southern states included in their notorious Black Codes a prohibition against blacks owning, or carrying, firearms. In congressional debates a number of congressmen specifically mentioned the denial of the right to armed self-defense as a reason for enacting the Fourteenth Amendment. Many of the twenty thousand plus state and local gun laws are probably violative of this section of the Constitution.

Notes on Chapter 1

1. William Marina, "Militia, Standing Armies and the Second Amendment," *Law and Liberty* (Spring 1976): 3.
2. Donald B. Kates, Jr., ed., *Restricting Handguns: The Liberal Skeptics Speak Out* (Croton-on-Hudson, N.Y.: North River Press, 1979), p.9.
3. Marina, op. cit., p. 3.
4. Kates, op. cit., p. 171.
5. Speech of January 7, 1790. Recorded in the *Boston Independent Chronicle*, January 14, 1790.
6. I *Writings of Thomas Paine* at 56 (1894).
7. Kates, op. cit., p. 10.
8. James E. Edwards, *Myths About Guns* (Coral Springs, Fla.: Peninsula Press, 1978), p. 97.
9. Unsigned article, *American Rifleman*, August 1977, p. 37.

10. Don Zutz, "The Intellectual Origins of the Second Amendment," *Rifle,* January-February 1973, p. 53.

11. *Webster's New World Dictionary,* College Edition, 1960, p933.

12. Ibid., p. 51.

13. Ibid.

14. Ibid., p. 52.

15. Ibid.

16. David Caplan, *Gun Week,* December 5, 1975, p. 4.

17. Kates, op. cit., p. 175.

Chapter 2

Gun Control: The Basic Issues

Is it true that law-enforcement officials oppose the right of the American people to possess weapons?

No, as the following statements from four major law-enforcement associations indicate.

International Association of Chiefs of Police--

"The International Association of Chiefs of Police supports the position that a citizen has a right, subject to state law, to own, acquire, and possess a handgun. The IACP hereby places itself on record as favoring legislation that supports mandatory minimum sentences for persons convicted of possessing or using a firearms during the commission of a crime."

National Sheriffs' Association--

"There is no valid evidence whatsoever to indicate that depriving law-abiding American citizens of the right to own arms would in any way lessen crime or criminal activity. The National Sheriffs' Association unequivocally opposes any legislation that has as its intent the confiscation of firearms or the taking away from law-abiding American citizens their right to purchase, own, and keep arms."

American Federation of Police--

"There are many Americans who fear for their lives. They know that often they will have to protect themselves, their own families, and their own property. Should these people be disarmed? There are enough laws. No, we don't need to disarm our loyal citizens, our friends, and our neighbors. We just need judges with the guts to make the use of a gun in a crime a risk that few will undertake in the future."

National Police Officers' Association of America--

"We feel that an American citizen of voting age and good character should have the right to purchase without restriction a handgun, pistol, revolver, rifle, shotgun, or like item without interference by a government body." [1]

Do American citizens have a right to self-defense?

The state constitutions of forty-three states guarantee citizens the right to use weapons in self-defense and that right is conferred statutorily in other states as well. Typical language of the forty-three states' views on this matter is that of Connecticut: "Every citizen has a right to bear arms in defense of himself and the state." [2]

Since handguns were registered in England in 1920, wouldn't similar laws bring about a reduction in crime in the United States?

According to Professor Donald B. Kates, "Although New York City firearms laws are much more stringent than England's, New York has far more violence. Conversely, Switzerland's firearms violence rate is minimal even though it has the world's highest per capita rate of gun possession among civilians." [3]

Since thousands of citizens die accidentally from firearms each year, shouldn't we try to eliminate the presence of these weapons?

A comprehensive study conducted by the National Safety Council shows that accidental death by firearms is near the bottom of the scale among causes of accidental death. The official rankings were (1) motor vehicles, (2) falls, (3) drowning, (4) burns, (5) poison, (6) suffocation, (7) firearms.[4] The same source also shows firearms accidents have decreased from 2,896 in 1967 to 1,800 in 1986.

Can firearms possession offer a means of self-defense for women?

Yes, according to Detective Jeanne Bray of the Columbus, Ohio, Police Department. In a television documentary Detective Bray cited a concerted police-citizen project to reduce rapes in the Orlando area. The police department offered a well-publicized training program in self-defense for women, and over six thousand women took part in the sessions. In the nine months following the training program there were just three rapes in Orlando--compared with thirty-three in the preceding nine months.[5]

If all guns aren't banned, shouldn't we at least eliminate the so-called Saturday night special?

One compelling argument against such a ban has been brought forward by Ernest Van den Haag. He reasons that both the poor and the elderly are the chief victims of crime and cannot necessarily afford expensive handguns for self-defense, and since inner-city police protection is so poor, many citizens must rely on self-protection.[6]

What would the cost be if the government embarks on a nationwide handgun confiscation program?

Aside from the cost of losing personal freedom, it is estimated that the cost of "buying back" confiscated handguns would be $10.8 billion.

The cost of a confiscation program would be astronomical. In November 1976 the voters of Massachusetts were given the opportunity to decide whether that state's inhabitants would continue to possess private handguns. A leader of the Massachusetts gun-ban organization, Middlesex County sheriff John J. Buckley, estimated that it could cost the Massachusetts taxpayers $300 million to buy back the gun owners' handguns. That price tag would cost every man, woman, and child in Massachusetts almost $53 apiece, and that cost did not cover rifles and shotguns, which the residents would be permitted to keep.

Should an attempt be made to confiscate all long guns, and since there are an estimated two to four times as many long guns as there are handguns, the $10.8 billion hand gun confiscation program would need to bear the additional long-gun confiscation costs of $21.6 billion to $43.2 billion. [7]

Do most opponents of gun control oppose all types of gun control?

Not all. The Citizens Committee for the Right to Keep and Bear Arms, for example, supports laws that deny the right to bear arms to those convicted of violent crimes, adjudicated mental incompetents, and other obvious examples of individuals who should not be granted the right to keep and bear arms. The National Rifle Association put forth a proposal to run instant backround checks on those wishing to purchase firearms. This system would identify those restricted by law from firearms ownership while not inconveniencing the law-abiding citizen.

Could strong gun-control measures really rid the nation of firearms?

It is highly doubtful that even a severe confiscation program could collect all the firearms in this nation. Former Attorney General Ramsey Clark has estimated that there may be as many as 200 million guns among the civilian population of this country. An attempt to exercise any form of gun control over them would be extremely difficult. Even relatively low-level legislation such as registration would cost several hundred million dollars at least. Confiscation and purchase, at an average of $50 each, would mean an expenditure of $10 billion. Furthermore, any such legislation would be seriously resisted by both criminals and those with strong moral objections such as this author. Even a two percent noncooperation rate (an extremely low figure) would mean that 4 million guns would be circulating throughout society. [8]

What are the general types of gun control in force in America today?

a. Control by prior official approval through a permit or licensing system.
b. Control by registration with a government agency.
c. Control by waiting period.
d. Control by simple restriction or prohibition. [9]

What is the object of those who support gun control or confiscation?

A sampling of direct quotes from proponents of gun control sheds some light on this question.

"Put simply, private citizens should be disarmed." *New Republic*

"No private citizen has any reason or need at any time to possess a gun. This applies to both honest citizens and criminals. We realize the Constitution guarantees the right to bear arms but this should be changed." *Detroit Daily Press*

"My personal choice for legislation is to remove all guns from private possession." Marvin E. Wolfgang, Chairman, Dept. of Sociology, University of Pennsylvania

"We seek a disarmed populace." *The Honest Politicians' Guide to Crime Control*

The Rights of Gun Owners

"Disarm America's private citizens--ourselves. This country needs a much stiffer gun-control law. Insist that all private ownership of guns be outlawed; that the guns now around be collected and destroyed." *Los Angeles Times* [10]

Does gun control really reduce the rate of violent crime?

Professor Donald B. Kates, writing in the *Civil Liberties Review*, cites a study conducted by the University of Wisconsin: "Gun-control laws have no individual or collective effect in reducing the rate of violent crime." The study took into account economic, demographic, racial, and other variables relating to gun-control effectiveness that could be quantified statistically.[11]

Wouldn't gun registration make it easier for law-enforcement officials to track down criminals?

No. For very important reasons: (1) If a criminal will disobey the law regarding some kind of crime, he will certainly not obey the law to register his weapon; (2) The Supreme Court of the U.S. has ruled in the *Haynes v. U.S.* decision in 1968 that criminals cannot be compelled to register their weapons because to do so would infringe on their Fifth Amendment right against self-incrimination.[12]

Is gun ownership the real cause of crime in America?

Not according to Congressman Bill Goodling (R-Pa.). Writing in *The Case Against the Reckless Congress*, Goodling says, "The American people understand that the willful criminal is the real cause of most violent crime--not the gun. They also understand that the tide of crime--the terrible threat of violence to our people--will not end until the prevailing attitude of those who refuse to reckon with that simple fact is changed. We should all be very concerned about the criminal use of firearms and we need legislation that will deal harshly with it. Mandatory sentencing is a step in the right direction, because the answer to the criminal use of firearms is not in gun prohibition, but in changing the way in which we deal with the people who commit crime.

"All of us would like to see crime reduced. But we need to be reasonable and practical when we assess the causes of crime, not emotional. The fact of the matter is, guns do not usually kill people unless people pull the triggers; any more than the presence of alcohol makes people alcoholics unless people drink it; or the presence of drugs makes people commit suicide unless someone willfully takes an overdose. Ultimately, people, not society or some inanimate object, are responsible for what goes on in this world." [13]

What is the best method to control criminal abuse of firearms if not through gun control?

Congressman Goodling, a widely respected expert on gun control and gun rights, has said that "instead of instituting gun control and thereby jeopardizing innocent citizens, we should be instituting sure and swift punishment for the most heinous of crimes. If potential criminals were assured that their deeds would result in swift, harsh, and irrevocable punishment, they would think twice before they trampled on someone else's rights. The eminent criminologist James Q. Wilson argues that sure, swift punishment--rather than increasing severity--is the key to crime control. That requires major court reform and revision of trial procedures so that the guilty do not escape conviction on technical grounds.

"It is time to bring justice into our judicial process. Few people would argue with the view that justice is denied if an innocent person is convicted. Fortunately, that does not happen very often. But justice is also denied if a person who commits an offense is allowed to go free, and such cases routinely occur in every court in the country. In fact, in numerous instances known criminals have been set free simply because complicated rules of evidence have seriously marred the American criminal justice system." [14]

Why do so many citizens and elected officials oppose gun registration and licensing?

Obviously many citizens fear that registration may be the forerunner of confiscation. One recent book, *The Gun in America,* offers some interesting insight into this question. "Though Americans own more firearms than ever before, they are increasingly unwilling to reveal that ownership to pollsters or others. It has been suggested that this fear is linked historically to the negative and distrustful attitudes toward government common when the Union was formed. Thus the gun owner fears the government will take away his gun and leave him defenseless against further inroads on his rights. Perhaps the fear of government itself does make all talk of registration like the touching of a raw nerve, but there may be an even more deeply rooted attitude about firearms that goes beyond considerations of society and government and touches the individual directly. Some years ago there was considerable discussion in the shooting press about the best 'survival gun.' This was not the weapon a man would choose if he were lost in the Rockies, but the one he should have with him when he crawled out of the rubble after a thermonuclear holocaust. With government, police, and courts gone, with social bonds dissolved, each man's survival would presumably depend on his wits, his strength, and his weapons. Such a spectacle may seem frightening or fanciful, but it reflects the persistent view that the ultimate defense of the individual American, his final, back-to-the-wall recourse, is his gun. The ultimate fear is not that government will tyrannize, but that it will fail to protect." [15]

Another view is offered by B. Bruce-Briggs: "At first

sight, licensing seems eminently reasonable. Dangerous criminals should not have weapons, nor should the mentally disturbed. But the administrative 'details' of licensing become incredibly difficult. It is fairly easy to check out an applicant for criminal record, which can be a legitimate reason for denying a license. But many criminals, judging from the comparison between reported crime and conviction rates, are not convicted of crimes, especially violent crimes, so the difficulty exists of whether to deny people the privilege of purchasing weapons if they have merely been arrested, but then set free or acquitted. Civil libertarians should be taken aback by this prospect. The question of mental competence is even nastier to handle. Is someone to be denied a firearm because he sought psychiatric help when his wife died?

"From the point of view of the organized gun owners, licensing is intolerable because of the way that it has been enforced in the past. One of the peculiarities of most local licensing is the lack of reciprocity; unlike marriage licensing, what is recognized in one jurisdiction is not in another." [16]

What are some of the positive steps to help stem both crime and criminal misuse of firearms?

The American Legislative Exchange Council (ALEC) has suggested model state legislation designed to address these problems. ALEC is a bipartisan organization of elected state legislators that is dedicated to helping legislators address problems of this nature. In *Suggested State Legislation*, published by ALEC, the following section was included in the criminal justice section:

Misuse of Firearms Control Act
        The suggested Misuse of Firearms Control Act is designed to prevent and punish the use of firearms to commit crimes while protecting the constitutional

right to keep and bear arms. It accomplishes this goal by requiring enhanced prison sentences for conviction for certain specially named crimes when committed with a firearm.

Laws which restrict or control ownership of firearms are not recommended, since such laws make it difficult or impossible for the defense of person and property.

Some states which require additional prison sentences for criminal use of firearms have seen dramatic reductions in the incidence of gun-related crimes. Arizona, for example, had a 21 percent reduction in armed robbery and other similar offenses since the suggested legislation was implemented two years ago.

Suggested Legislation
(Title, enacting clause, etc.)

Section 1. (Short title.) This act may be cited as the Misuse of Firearms Control Act.

Section 2. (Additional penalties for possession of a firearms or explosive device in the commission of certain crimes.) Notwithstanding any other provision of law to the contrary, any person who uses a firearm or explosive device at the time he commits or attempts to commit the crime of murder, aggravated rape, kidnapping, manslaughter, aggravated battery, simple kidnapping, aggravated escape, aggravated burglary, or aggravated arson (or other appropriate offenses) shall upon conviction serve a term of two years imprisonment for the first conviction. Upon conviction for each second and subsequent offense listed in this section, he shall serve a term of five years' imprisonment. The penalty provided herein shall be in addition to any other penalty imposed under the provisions of law, and such a person shall serve the additional term of imprisonment without benefit of parole, probation, suspension of sentence, or credit for good time, and any adjudication of guilt or imposition of sentence shall not be suspended.

The prison terms provided under the provisions of this section shall run consecutively to any other penalty imposed upon conviction of any of the crimes listed in this section.

Section 3. (Severability clause.)
Section 4. (Repealer clause.)
Section 5. (Effective date.) [17]

If a handgun ban were instituted, is there any evidence that citizens would comply with such a law?

As a matter of fact there is startling evidence to the contrary. Despite extremely stringent laws regarding possession of firearms in New York City, experts estimate that there are some two million handguns illegally owned in New York City. It appears unlikely, therefore, that similar bans would be enforceable.

One recent estimate, taking the form of a report to the governor of Massachusetts, states that a minimum of 100,000 citizens would defy a handgun ban in that state. Further, one national poll indicates that approximately half of the American gun owners can be expected to defy any such banning legislation. [18]

What are some of the obvious difficulties facing any gun law?

David Hardy, a noted authority on gun laws, has observed in a recent rebuttal to the General Accounting Office that any gun-control law is doomed to failure for the following reasons:

1. Evasion by thefts: BATF has already established that 20-25 percent of the criminal arsenal is *even now* composed of stolen guns.
2. Homemade or "zip" guns, fashioned from

pipe and wood, or cap guns: authorities have found these produced by the hundreds in strict gun-control regions.

3. Use of other weapons--knives and clubs--for the same lethal purpose.

4. The difficulty of predicting future murderers: it has been shown that neither criminal records, nor commitments, nor psychiatric testing has any success in predicting future violence. The comptroller's claim that most murderers have "criminal records" is misleading: first, the sample only lists murderers with at least one federal arrest (since murder is rarely a federal crime, most of those with no record are excluded); second, it lists arrests rather than convictions.

5. To the extent that controls are aimed at handguns, evasion by use of long arms is always possible: moreover, such arms can be easily "sawed off"-- probably with less effort than a person now goes to if he travels to another state to purchase. [19]

Do areas with strict firearms control have reduced homicide rates?

No, in fact it has been established that twenty percent of American homicides occur in four U.S. cities that make up only six-percent of the population. The four cities-- New York, Washington, D.C., Detroit, and Chicago--have the nation's toughest gun laws in force and still have extremely high homicide rates. [20]

David Hardy, after an exhaustive review of firearms ownership and homicide rates, concludes his study by stating that the "imposition of nationwide firearm controls would not have a significant impact upon homicide rates. The experience of existing controls, whether assessed by simple comparisons or by elaborate statistical tools, does not indicate that existing controls have had a measurable influence upon homicide rates. Additional controls would face serious impediments due to the difficulty of predicting future killers, illegal firearm markets, improvised firearms, and substitute weapons. These impediments, complicated by the mass of firearms involved, form significant barriers to the effectiveness of any system of firearm controls." [21]

How many gun-control ordinances are there? What do they do?

According to reputable sources, including noted gun authority B. Bruce-Briggs, there are some twenty thousand gun-control ordinances in the United States today. According to Bruce-Briggs, most are "prohibitions against discharging a weapon in urban areas or against children carrying weapons, and are trivial, reasonable, and uncontroversial. Most states and large cities have laws against carrying concealed weapons, the rationale being that no person has a legitimate reason to do so. In a few large cities and states, particularly in the Northeast, a license is required to buy or possess a handgun, and in very few but growing number of northeastern cities and states a permit or license is required to possess any sort of firearm." [22]

The increase in the number of such ordinances proposed annually is something that does cause considerable alarm to proponents of Second Amendment rights.

Massachusetts enacted one of the nation's most stringent firearms control laws, and that act has been in force since 1975. How has this law impacted the homicide rate in Massachusetts?

According to a recently published critique of the Massachusetts law, that legislation has not had a long-term effect in discouraging homicides.

Between January and September of 1979 the homicide

rate in the six largest Massachusetts cities (population over 100,000) increased by twenty-two percent over that of the previous year. That increase was double the national average.

Additionally, the *New York Daily News*, in its analysis of the measure, stated: "Boston police and Massachusetts law-enforcement officials say the law is generally working as a deterrent to some gun crimes, although its impact on hardened criminals is minimal." Bartley-Fox's impact was minimized by Michael Donovan, spokesman for the Boston Police Department: "The criminal element still has guns available. We have young white gangs in our Charlestown area who are using guns to hold up banks. It has had no effect on them at all." After three years of Bartley-Fox, in 1978 Massachusetts ranked as the thirteenth most-robbery-prone state in America, and the eighteenth most-aggravated-assault-prone state. Over the period 1975-78, its aggravated-assault cases rose thirty-seven percent in number, making it the fifth fastest-growing assault state, about twice the national average. [23]

What kind of legislation do gun owners and pro-gun organizations support to counter the impact of the 1968 Gun Control Act?

Although there have been numerous bills introduced to reform or repeal provisions of the 1968 act, the most serious measures were introduced by Sen. James A. McClure (R-Id.) and by Rep. Harold Volkmer (D-Mo.). This legislation, which was passed in 1986, reformed portions of the 1968 Gun Control Act by:

1. Allowing congressional review of Bureau of Alcohol, Tobacco and Firearms regulations;
2. Loosening restrictions on firearms sales by individuals;
3. Banning seizures of firearms without lawful arrest;

4. Allowing purchases of long arms across state lines if the purchase is legal in both states;

5. Limiting current law prohibiting gun ownership to those convicted of or indicted for a felony, to those convicted of a felony.

This legislation has been called "absolutely essential to maintain the rights of America's gun owners." [24]

What are some general statistics regarding gun ownership in America?

Over half of the American people own guns to protect themselves and their loved ones from crime, according to a recent survey conducted by Research & Associates, Inc., for A-T-O, Inc. This suggests strongly that the majority of our citizens view general gun ownership not as a coefficient of crime but as a coefficient of protection against criminal activity.

The survey, *The Figgie Report on Fear of Crime: America Afraid,* published in 1980, was based on a random sampling of 1,047 digit-dial telephones in the continental United States. It indicates that:

· People living outside large cities, particularly those living in rural areas, are the most likely to own guns. Sixty-two percent of rural households have guns, compared with 42 percent of the households in the large metropolitan areas, 54 percent of small-city residents, and 51 percent of suburbanites.

· Sixty-nine percent of the people in the South have guns in their households, as do 52 percent in the Midwest, 51 in the West, and 31 percent in the East.

· Sixty percent of the married people own guns, compared with 45 percent of the single people and 36 percent of those previously married.

· Fifty-nine percent of the males have guns as do 45 percent of all females. However, divorced, separated, or widowed women are far more likely to own guns than are previously married men, figures being 68 percent and 32 percent, respectively.

· Fifty percent of those under fifty years of age own their own guns while 45 percent of those over fifty do.

· Blacks (58 percent) more often have a gun in their homes than do whites (51 percent).

· Those who see frequent reports about crime in the newspapers and on TV are more likely to be gun owners than those who do not. Fifty-five percent of those who say they see crime reports daily on TV own guns, compared with 45 percent who see such reports less frequently. Similarly, 54 percent of those who read crime-related articles daily in the newspaper have household guns, as do 48 percent of those who read such articles less frequently.

What is the attitude of America's gun owners toward federal firearms legislation?

Although no conclusive study has been conducted, the Second Amendment Foundation's 1989 "Gun Owners Survey"[25] found that, of the over 250,000 participants:

* Do you oppose granting the Secretary of the Treasury the right to ban guns? 98 percent responded "yes."

* Do you oppose a national law requiring a seven day waiting period before you can buy a gun? 91 percent responded "yes."

* Do you oppose Congressional attempts to ban all fully-automatic firearms? 89 percent responded "yes."

* Do you oppose all attempts to ban semi-automatic firearms? 91 percent responded "yes."

* Do you oppose all attempts to restrict handgun ownership by law-abiding citizens? 92 percent responded "yes."

* Do you oppose a ban on all .25 and .32 ammunition? 96 percent responded "yes."

Have the very tough gun-control laws in England been a help or a hindrance toward reducing crime?

According to Superintendent Colin Greenwood of the West Yorkshire Constabulary, "The gun-control laws, despite what we all believed--and I believed too--have had no effect on serious crime at all. They have not reduced as far as one can see the number of illegal firearms....It's a complete waste of time." [26]

Notes on Chapter 2

1. Congressman J. Kenneth Robinson, "Is Gun Control Constitutional?" *Can You Afford this House?* ed. David C. Treen (Ottawa, Ill.: Green Hill Publishers, 1978), p. 93.

2. James E. Edwards, *Myths About Guns* (Coral Springs Fla.: Peninsula Press, 1978), p. 91.

3. Donald B. Kates, Jr., *The Great Gun Control Debate* (Bellevue, Wash.: Second Amendment Foundation, 1977).

4. National Safety Council, *Accident Facts,* 1987 Edition, charts, pp. 6-7 and p. 20.

5. Transcript of "The Gun Grabbers," television documentary produced by the Citizens Committee for the Right to Keep and Bear Arms (Bellevue, Wash., 1978), p. 9.

6. Ernest Van den Haag, "Banning Handguns-Helping the Criminal Hurt You," *New Woman,* November-December 1975, p. 80.

7. *The Saturday Night Special--Why It Should Not Be Banned* (Bellevue, Wash.: Second Amendment Foundation, 1978), p. 9.

8. Jeffrey D. Kane, *The Case Against Gun Control* (Bellevue, Wash.: Second Amendment Foundation, 1977), p. 7.

9. Edwards, op. cit., p. 27.

10. Robert J. Kukla, *Gun Control* (Harrisburg, Pa.: Stackpole Books, 1973).

11. Kane, op. cit., pp. 6-7.

12. Kukla, op. cit., p. 18.

13. Congressman Bill Goodling, "The Disarming of Citizens," *The Case Against the Reckless Congress,* ed. Marjorie Holt (Ottawa, Ill.: Green Hill Publishers, 1976), pp. 71-72.

14. Ibid., p. 75.

15. Lee Kennett, *The Gun in America* (Westport, Conn.: Greenwood Press, 1975), pp. 253-254.

16. B. Bruce-Briggs, *The Great American Gun War* (Bellevue, Wash.: Second Amendment Foundation, 1977), p. 7.

17. 1978-79 *Suggested State Legislation,* ed. Donna J. Carlson (Washington, D.C.: American Legislative Exchange Council, 1977), pp. 35-38.

18. David T. Hardy, *No Case for Stricter Handgun Control* (Bellevue, Wash.: Second Amendment Foundation, 1978), pp. 15-16.

19. Ibid., p. 9.

20. Ibid., p. 3.

21. David T. Hardy and John Stompoly, *Of Arms and the Law* (Bellevue, Wash.: Second Amendment Foundation, 1976), p. 53.

22. B. Bruce-Briggs, *The Great American Gun War* (Bellevue, Wash.: Second Amendment Foundation, 1977), *p. 7.*

23. *Mandatory Sentencing for Handgun Possession: A Critique of the Bartley-Fox Law* (Bellevue, Wash.: Second Amendment Foundation, 1980), pp. 2-3.

24. "Federal Firearms Reform Act," *Point Blank,* ed. John M. Snyder, October 1979, pp. 4-5.

25. Second Amendment Foundation Survey, unpublished. The survey was conducted throughout 1989.

26. "Gun Week Self-Improvement Test," *Gun Week,* vol. 15 issue 697, p. 16.

Chapter 3

BATF Abuse of
Gun Owners Rights

*W*HAT IS BATF?

"BATF" stands for Bureau of Alcohol, Tobacco and Firearms, a division of the United States Department of Treasury. The bureau, also known as ATF, was formerly a subdivision of the Internal Revenue Service, when it was known as the ATF Division. The bureau was given independent status within the Department of Treasury in 1972.

What is the function of BATF?

As its relationship to the IRS would indicate, BATF is primarily a tax-collection agency, specializing in commerce that is heavily taxed and otherwise regulated by the government: alcohol, tobacco, and firearms. Historically, one of the key activities of the bureau has been locating and destroying moonshine stills.

Does BATF still engage in this kind of revenue enforcement?

To a limited extent. Before 1969 tobacco and alcohol were the only significant responsibilities of the bureau, and "enforcement of federal tobacco taxes had never required significant effort."[1] Deployment of agents in 1968 was primarily in the area of alcohol enforcement. In that year the bureau made 5,400 arrests, of which only 450 were for firearms violations.[2]

Did this change in 1969?

Yes. With the passage of the Gun Control Act of 1968 (GCA), responsibility for enforcing the increasing federal regulation of firearms fell into the hands of BATF. It was at this time that the term "firearms" was appended to the Alcohol and Tobacco Division of the IRS, later to become BATF. Other changes came in the early seventies as the price of sugar, a major component in moonshine, increased threefold. The result was a 250 percent increase in the price of illegal alcohol, rendering it incapable of competition with the regulated distilleries. Between 1972 and 1978 the number of stills raided fell from 2,981 to 361.[3]

What are the primary tenets of the GCA, which BATF enforces?

The requirement that all dealer sales be recorded on special Treasury forms; the expansion of the class of persons prohibited from buying guns to include not only felons, but also persons not residing in the state in which the sale is being made (also drug users, those with dishonorable military discharges, and other categories); the banning of virtually all interstate firearms sales except between two dealers; and expansion of the $200 excise tax and permit requirements on machineguns and other special weapons to include a category called "destructive devices."

What happened to BATF agents who formerly worked in alcohol enforcement?

For the most part, they were transferred to firearms enforcement, still a growing area of bureau activity. Even this shift provided many fewer agents for firearms enforcement than were necessary to regulate law-abiding gun owners with the zeal desired by many bureaucrats. At the same time, the number of agents was far greater than was required to handle the genuine criminal offenses being committed.

How did BATF deal with this contradiction?

By using a simple but ingenious method. Through meticulous regulation of licensed dealers, combined with criminal prosecution of licensees, collectors, and others who never intended to violate the law, the bureau undertook to create impressive arrest statistics for itself, while working toward a publicly stated goal of driving 129,000 licensed dealers out of business,[4] to make the job of regulation "easier for BATF's outnumbered forces."[5]

How can people who never meant to violate the law be prosecuted?

First GCA specifies that criminal intent does not have to be proved for a felony conviction. It is necessary only that one of the numerous technical violations under GCA be committed. That this violation may have been an accident or that the dealer or citizen was led into the violation through entrapment is no defense.

What is entrapment?

Entrapment is a method by which the suspect is lured, tricked, or encouraged to commit a crime by the government, so that he can then be arrested. The plea that a defendant has been persuaded or tricked into committing a crime that he did not intend is an affirmative defense under many statutes. The limits of legal entrapment were drawn by the Supreme Court in 1932, when it ruled: "The first duties of the officers of the law are to prevent, not to punish crime. It is not their duty to incite crime. Decoys may be used to entrap criminals, and to present opportunity to one intending to commit crime. But decoys are not permissible to ensnare the innocent and the law-abiding into the commission of a crime."[6] BATF uses such ensnarement against both licensed dealers and average gun owners-collectors.

How does entrapment against gun collectors work?

The law requires that a license be obtained by anyone "engaged in the business" of dealing in firearms. The statute, however, does not define "dealing," and BATF has made no effort to define the term until recently. Historically, the bureau has stated that persons who sell "four to six" guns a year do not need a license. In fact, such persons are discouraged from applying for licenses, since issuing them would result in more regulatory work for BATF. Yet, despite these assurances, the bureau has prosecuted many collectors who have done no more than sell that small number of guns.

Entrapment proceeds in this way: A government agent will approach a collector or other private seller and purchase a gun. The agent then may make subsequent purchases at gun shows or other occasions, and will then arrest the seller for "dealing without a license."

Can this be done even if the number of guns sold was less than four to six?

Yes. Despite the statements of BATF that a few sales are permissible, a BATF memo was introduced at a Senate hearing into bureau operations which suggested that "a single [gun] sale or act may constitute engaging in the business" of dealing in firearms.[7] When the Second Amendment Foundation conducted its Task Force to Investigate the Enforcement Policies of BATF, we received this testimony from a former BATF agent who had worked in the Montana regional office: "It was a common joke that whenever a gun owner telephoned our office inquiring about how he could comply with BATF regulations, agents would provide false answers to the inquiries, ask who they were, and then set them up in entrapment situations to arrest them for illegal selling of firearms."[8]

Are other kinds of entrapment used by BATF?

One method used to arrest licensed dealers is known as a straw-man sale. This sale hinges upon the fact that dealers may not sell to certain "prohibited persons" — nonresidents of their state, persons under a certain age, felons, and others. At the same time, it is common for one individual legally to buy for another who might himself be prohibited from purchase. An adult, for example, purchases for a juvenile, or an out-of-state dealer makes a purchase so that a resident of his state may then purchase from him.

In the straw-man entrapment an agent or an informant who is a prohibited person approaches a dealer to buy a firearm. The agent then produces out-of-state identification or indicates that he cannot sign the registration form (which contains a statement that he is not a prohibited person). The dealer invariably refuses to sell.

The "prohibited person" then suggests that someone else (usually a local friend or relative) could purchase the gun for him. If the dealer takes the bait, he will respond that he can sell to a local person, provided that person can produce valid local identification and can legally fill out the purchase forms.

The prohibited person then returns with a second agent, the straw man. The straw man produces the required identification and signs the appropriate forms. The prohibited person, however, is the one who comes up with the money; at the end of the transaction the straw man steps back and the prohibited person quickly steps in to pick up the firearm. The dealer is then arrested for selling to a prohibited person.

If BATF believes this kind of sale improper, why does it not merely send out a notice informing dealers that this is the case?

The intention of BATF has obviously not been to prevent violations of the law. On the contrary, it is interested in creating violations of the law, if these "crimes" can then be quickly solved and added to the bureau's arrest statistics. Following hearings before a Senate appropriations subcommittee, BATF director G.R. Dickerson informed the subcommittee chairman, Senator Dennis DeConcini (D-Ariz.), that "we have developed an industry circular which will be distributed to federal firearms licensees explaining the 'straw-man transaction' and the responsibilities of the licensees under the Gun Control Act."[9] It should be noted that this rather obvious move came only after the bureau was severely criticized during the hearing for its failures in this area.

Are there other forms of entrapment?

Yes, BATF has been involved in some questionable activities related to machineguns, particularly deactivated war trophies ("Dewats"). BATF has provided information on how legally to deactivate certain fully automatic weapons (through welding) so that they may not be "readily restored" to full auto operation. The information it provides, however, is different from the legal requirements for deactivation which it introduces at the trial of those who follow its advice.

A related episode occurred when a company in Georgia began selling submachinegun parts that had been made inoperative according to BATF requirements: the critical lower receiver had been torch-cut into three to five pieces. This was fine with the bureau until, according to BATF, rewelded submachineguns began being used in crime. At this point BATF agents began contacting all those who had bought parts from the Atlanta company, and demanded that they be surrendered. In later hearings before the House Subcommittee on Crime, John Ashbrook (R-Ohio) charged that BATF had purposely approved the sale of the demilitarized receiver parts, knowing all along that it would eventually go out and confiscate the parts from purchasers.

Why would BATF do that?

Like any other bureau entrapment effort, this effort was undertaken to boost statistics. By allying itself with the sellers of illegal machinegun parts, BATF was effortlessly about to boost its statistics for confiscated fully automatic weapons. Similarly, all of the bureau's entrapment efforts are directed toward building a record of arrests by which to justify its existence. But even with its manufactured cases, BATF has an extremely low productivity level. The bureau spends approximately $70,000 per case, with a ratio, including large-scale entrapment, of less than one case per year per agent.[10] Because of the danger or difficulty of doing so, the BATF prefers not actively to penetrate criminal firearms markets.

Are these the only improper actions of BATF?

Unfortunately, no. Closely related to the issue of entrapment, although quite rare, have been examples of extortion used by the bureau against those it hoped to arrest. In one case, agents implied that they had Mafia connections, and that it would be unhealthy for the dealer not to buy a $5,000 shipment of illegal weapons. When he did so, he was arrested and subsequently convicted. One BATF agent was fired and convicted of extortion after he paid informants to beat a prospective buyer until the man would make an illegal firearms purchase and be arrested.[11]

Are there other examples of abuses more sanctioned by BATF policy than cases of actual extortion?

Warrantless searches, primarily of dealers, are an area of great concern. In the area of search and entry, the Bureau of Alcohol, Tobacco and Firearms enjoys distinct advantages over most law-enforcement agencies. At least where dealers' premises are concerned, the bureau is statutorily permitted broad search powers without the necessity of probable causes or warrant. Under the 1968 Gun Control Act, agents of the Treasury "may enter during business hours the premises (including places of storage) of any firearms or ammunition dealer for the purpose of examining or inspecting (1) any records or documents required to be kept by such licensed importer, licensed manufacturer, licensed dealer, or licensed collector under this chapter or rules or regulations under this chapter and (2) any firearms or ammunition kept or stored, by such licensed importer, licensed manufacturer, licensed dealer, or licensed collector at such premises."[12]

Doesn't that violate the Fourth Amendment's requirement that warrantless searches be made only upon probable cause?
   Normally, the Constitution does require that searches (1) be reasonable; that is, based upon probable cause—information that would persuade a reasonable man that a crime probably has been committed and that the place to be searched contains evidence—and (2) be supported by a warrant (with limited exceptions for emergency situations). The warrant requirement is critical; it ensures that before the search is made, a neutral judicial official must be persuaded that a basis exists. Moreover, since the warrant must describe particularly the place to be searched and the items to be seized, it prevents the search from becoming a "fishing expedition" and enables the person on the receiving end to know how far the searchers may go.

Do BATF searches fall under one of the "limited exceptions"?
   Yes. These exceptions include criminal matters like "hot pursuit" into a building and "stop-and-frisk" situations of persons in the open.[13] Most important, there is an exception for administrative searches. Such searches were upheld for building code inspections in 1967,[14] and under

GCA '68 in 1972.[15]

What did the Supreme Court Say about the legality of administrative searches under GCA '68?

The Court agreed that the searches were proper, saying:

It is apparent that if the law is to be properly enforced and inspection made effective, inspections without warrant must be deemed reasonable conduct under the Fourth Amendment. Unannounced, even frequent, inspections are essential. In this context, the prerequisite of a warrant could easily frustrate inspection.

It is also plain that inspections for compliance with the Gun Control Act pose only limited threats to the dealer's justifiable expectations of privacy. When a dealer chooses to engage in this pervasively regulated business and to accept a federal license, he does so with the knowledge that his business records, firearms, and ammunition will be subject to inspection.[16]

Was this the Supreme Court's last word on the subject?

Directly, yes. However, six years after the above decision the Court did recognize limits upon the extent of this doctrine. In *Marshall v. Barlow* [17] the Court held that administrative searches under the Occupational Safety and Health Act (OSHA) could not be conducted without warrants. That act permitted search of the work area of virtually every business whose products affect interstate commerce. The Court noted that "the warrant clause of the Fourth Amendment protects commercial buildings as well as private homes." Nonetheless, although it struck down warrantless OSHA searches, it reaffirmed its holding that warrantless Gun Control Act searches were constitutional: "Certain industries have such a history of government oversight that no reasonable expectation of privacy could exist for a proprietor.Liquor and firearms are industries of this type."[18]

The concept that firearms dealerships have been subject to long-term comprehensive control ignores several facts. The Gun Control Act regulation is hardly long-term; most of it was but four years old in 1972, when *Biswell* was decided (in contrast, OSHA had reached the ripe old age of eight by the 1978 *Marshall* ruling). It is hardly so pervasive that one engaging in it forfeits all notions of privacy (the 1968 act indeed contains, in its statement of purpose, elaborate pronouncements that it was not intended to interfere with peaceful ownership or use of firearms, nor was it to impose unreasonable burdens on the same.)

How do dealers feel about these warrantless searches?

Generally, dealers have accepted routine inspections and searches as normal and have directed most of their complaints to those cases in which agents have gone beyond the norm in their search, or have conducted raids.[19]

How is a raid different from a search?

Although the raid would normally include a search, the term "raid" is used here to indicate a large-scale criminal enforcement operation, as opposed to routine administrative inspections. BATF's manual on the subject defines "raid" as "the sudden appearance by officers for the purpose of arresting law violators and seizing contraband."

Is BATF's conduct in raids also a matter of concern to law-abiding gun owners?

Very much so. Many examples are available of raids in which agents have clearly gone too far in dealing with supposed criminals—who were actually honest citizens.

- Silver Spring, Maryland, June 1971: Four plainclothes government agents broke down the back door of the apartment of Ken Ballew, who was in the bathtub at the time. Ballew armed himself with an antique revolver and prepared to defend himself against what he thought were criminals. He was shot by the agents and suffered permanent brain damage and paralysis as a result.
- San Jose, California, June 1978: Twenty armed government agents raided a collectors show, allowing no one to leave for two hours. The agents photographed exhibitors and by standers and forced everyone present to sign "warning forms."
- Kirkland, Washington, October 1978: In a paramilitary-style operation, government agents invaded the neighborhood of Mr. and Mrs. Elmer Turngren. A four-block area was sealed off, the neighborhood evacuated, and the Turngren home surrounded. Some of the agents ransacked their home, while others stood over the family with automatic rifles. At the time of the raid, Mr. Turngren had been asleep and his wife was reading a Bible lesson. The only other person living there was their grade-school-aged daughter.

These are all shocking cases, but are they isolated incidents?

Definitely not. Although the bureau's manual *Raids and Searches* has been released only in a censored form, those portions that have not been suppressed are enough to indicate that many improper actions of BATF are not the aberrations of individual, overzealous agents, but matters of official policy.

Although federal judge Whitman Knapp ruled that certain portions of the manual must be disclosed, he agreed with the bureau's arguments that disclosure of some sections could hinder investigations. At the same time he expressed reservations about some of the information he had discovered during his inspection of the manual.

"Some withheld sections describe enforcement techniques which are of dubious legality under the Fourth Amendment," Knapp wrote. "Although we do not decide whether any techniques are unconstitutional, we do note our grave doubts with respect to some of them."[20]

Additionally, during the first congressional hearings into BATF activities, before a subcommittee of the Senate Appropriations Committee, a study was presented that indicated a pattern of BATF abuses toward honest citizens.

Former U.S. Customs commissioner Vernon Acree, called the "dean of Treasury law enforcement" at the time of his retirement, was retained by progun forces to study a large number of BATF cases to determine their law-enforcement value.

Acree testified that after investigating every BATF prosecution filed in the Maryland and Virginia federal districts during a two-year period, it was his opinion that BATF was concerned more with building an arrest record than with cutting crime. The bureau's activity, according to Acree, "smacks of a statistical rat-race kind of operation.In my judgement [75 to 80 percent of these] individuals would not have fallen into the hands of the law, had they not been enticed, inveigled, and encouraged to violate some provision of the law which they were totally unfamiliar with."[21]

What have been the bureau's actions following searches and raids?

Usually a raid is immediately followed by the seizure of an entire firearms collection or dealer's inventory, and then by BATF's attempts to force the defendant to forfeit his property.

The bureau is statutorily authorized, as part of its enforcement powers, to seize and forfeit firearms which it can establish were "involved in or used or intended to be used" in violation of the 1968 act or of any other federal criminal statute. Those provisions are holdovers from the days when BATF was part of the IRS, and are cross-referenced with Internal Revenue Code.

The power to seize private property associated with statutory violation is not unique to the 1968 act. Agents have long used similar statutes to seize not only illegal commodities such as smuggled goods, but also the vehicles that have transported such commodities.

How does BATF benefit from such seizures?

The forfeiture is technically civil, not criminal, so the government need not prove its case beyond a reasonable doubt—some courts have even held that evidence illegally obtained may be used to prove the government's case. And although a person cannot be fined before trial, a seizure can be made instantly, leaving to the owner the burden of obtaining the property. The seizure also imposes an economic hardship on a defendant. Before trial, it reduces his chance to sell the property or obtain a loan on it, reducing his economic ability to fight back. After the trial, he is put to the expense of a second trial, a civil trial, to regain his property.

Just how many guns does BATF confiscate or require forfeiture of?

BATF appears to utilize the seizure and forfeiture power much more than do other governmental agencies with similar powers. From October 1, 1983 to September 30, 1989, the BATF seized 69,043 firearms. In economic terms, we can conservatively estimate the seizures to have been worth $8.1 million.

Were these guns of a kind particularly suited to street crime?

No. Records obtained from BATF through the Freedom

of Information Act indicate that the bureau has little appetite for confiscating the kind of firearms it insists are most used in crime—handguns, especially Saturday night specials. Only 47.7 percent of the confiscated firearms during our study period were handguns, and *only 4.04 percent were Saturday night specials,* by the BATF's own definition. In contrast, expensive collectors' items appeared frequently in the records.[23]

How is it that BATF can refuse to return firearms, even after a defendant is acquitted of all charges?

BATF argues that acquittal in a criminal action does not prevent the bureau from seeking, in a civil action, to forfeit a collection of firearms on exactly the same grounds. As noted above, this route is particularly easy for BATF, since the government does not have to prove its case beyond a reasonable doubt.

The bureau has been able to force these double trials by adopting a subtle inconsistency. Under traditional forms of forfeiture (primarily for violation of federal laws on untaxed liquor and narcotics) the courts treated the civil suit as "remedial" rather than "punitive." In other words, the government has lost large amount of tax money, and was thus entitled to a civil remedy of keeping vehicles, to be auctioned off, as compensation for lost tax revenue.

Yet the revenue damages to the government in dealing-without-a-license cases are minimal—all that is lost is the $10 license fee. Additionally, many of these people willingly would have become dealers so that they could legally transfer a small number of firearms, except that BATF inconsistently states that no such license is necessary to sell a few guns, and will not issue one. The forfeiture, therefore, is intended to punish the firearm owner, *not* to restore lost government revenue by a remedial civil action.[24]

How does BATF decide who to raid?

Two issues are of concern here: the use of informants

and the matter of law-enforcement "targeting." Targeting concerns itself with which lawbreakers, of all of those who may be committing crimes, a law-enforcement agency will devote its time to. In the case of the BATF, priority is given not to those committing serious crime, but randomly, or to honest dealers who can be entrapped as targets of opportunity. In a number of cased, prosecutions have been instigated against persons against who BATF held some special grudge, such as those too scrupulous to inform upon their friends. In one such case, agents spent 1,000 hours trying to find a sufficient charge for arresting a particular dealer. This is ironic, because for several years bureau administrators have complained to Congress that they don't have enough funds to enforce federal gun laws or to move against gun thefts, which make up twenty-two percent of guns used in crime.[25] Most of the cases discussed as examples of abusive raids were originally matters of improper targeting: in each case money and time were expended against those with no criminal intent. In at least one case—that of Ken Ballew—the results were tragic.

What about BATF's use of informants?

This is a questionable area in all law enforcement, but one that BATF has taken to the limits of what the courts will tolerate. The use of informants is regarded as undesirable, because, in the words of one judge, informants are often "without scruples of any kind."[26] Given the slightest reason to do so, they have no compunction about lying to judge and jury. More important, BATF often presents them with a motive to lie: contingency payments.

What are contingency payments?

Payments to an informant for the prosecution only if his information results in arrest or conviction. Not surprisingly, many informants are willing to say most anything to ensure conviction. Although the American Bar Association holds it unethical for an attorney to acquiesce in such contingency-witness payments because they encourage frame-ups, and are a substantial inducement to perjury, BATF nonetheless engages in such practice in its attempt to boost its conviction rate.

In one instance in 1978, a New York judge dismissed such a case, noting: "BATF provided him with an economic motive for producing arrests; BATF failed to take steps to ensure the reliability of the informants version of the events."[27] Concluded the judge, "We believe that the criminal defendant is needlessly exposed to unacceptable risk of a serious miscarriage of justice and this trial should not be permitted to continue."[28] In another case, the court noted that such contingency fees are "essentially revolting to an ordered society."[29]

Why haven't these events received some publicity?

In a sense, they have. BATF has received more than its share of good publicity. Much of this, of course, traces to media bias in favor of gun control; those who enforce the gun laws are naturally seen as an asset to society. But good press also has been achieved through the heavy attention BATF accords media relations. The bureau's manual *Public Affairs Guidelines* advises administrative agents to "cultivate and maintain news media contacts." Special agents in charge and chiefs of field operations are "required to submit as quickly as possible" duplicate copies of all news and magazine articles mentioning BATF. Photographs of BATF operations should "be 'action'-oriented as opposed to the evidence-type photographs needed for case report work."[30]

Don't most police agencies have such public relations programs?

Yes, and there is nothing inherently wrong with an effective press relations program. It deserves condemnation, however, when its purpose is not to inform the public, but to further the case against a defendant. BATF has a distinct preference for releasing information detrimental to one accused.

In his introduction to *Public Affairs Guidelines*, former BATF director Rex Davis noted that "an effective public affairs program has a favorable impact on the attitude of the court, jurors, and prosecutors"[31] What passes as press relations might be more accurately styled indirect jury tampering.

Trial by press is a popular method against those against whom BATF has a weak case. Although the manual states that "under no circumstances" should agents comment upon a defendant's character and record or voice opinions about his guilt, those proscriptions are often ignored.

Have any of these many improper actions drawn the attention of Congress?

Yes. Following a great deal of independent collection of evidence, and some pressure on Congress, hearings into BATF were held before committees chaired by Sen. Dennis DeConcini (D-Ariz.), Rep. John Conyers (D-Mich.), and Sen. Birch Bayh (D-Ind.). The hearings before Conyers' House Subcommittee on Crime were a sham; the antigun Conyers allowed testimony about an unrelated bill to ban Saturday night specials and from the National Coalition to Ban Handguns, while seeking to prevent progun members of the committee, particularly John Ashbrook (R-Ohio), from effectively questioning the witnesses. Hearings before DeConcini and Bayh, however, probed the many allegations of BATF misbehavior.

Will Congress do anything more than hold hearings into BATF activities?

In a sense, it has. The Firearms Owners' Protection Act of 1986 was signed into law by Ronald Reagan. The Act sought to reduce BATF abuses of power by addressing several problem areas:

It defined firearms "dealer,"[32] a definition the

BATF was unwilling to make until it was so criticized during hearings before a Senate appropriations subcommittee that it was forced to act. Such a definition reduced BATF's opportunities to entrap law-abiding gun collectors for "dealing without a license," or some other trumped-up charge.

It required reasonable grounds for a search before a federally licensed dealer's premises may be entered to inspect records and inventory.[33]

It prohibitted the common practice by BATF of seizing all firearms from an individual. The bill would allow only those guns directly involved in an alleged violation of the law to be seized.

It required the return of firearms by BATF if the individual is acquitted, charges are dropped, or the court so orders. As discussed above, BATF has previously held that acquittal did not require it to return a dealer's inventory, a notion that does not fit with traditional notions of justice in America.

It provided that a qualified individual could purchase a long firearm in any state, if such a transaction is legal under local laws.

It provided a legislative review of regulations propagated by BATF, by requiring a ninety-day comment period on any proposed firearms rule.[34]

Despite these reforms, BATF still has violated the rights of law-abiding gun owners. Groups such as the Citizens Committee for the Right to Keep and Bear Arms, the National Rifle Association, and the Second Amendment Foundation continually find themselves requested to aid in the defense of a law-abiding person trapped by BATF enforcement of gun laws.

Notes on Chapter 3

1. David T. Hardy, *The BATF's War on Civil Liberties: The Assault on Gun Owners* (Bellevue, Wash.: Second Amendment Foundation. 1979), p. 7.
2. Ibid.
3. Ibid, pp. 7-8.
4. Rex Davis, former BATF director, speaking to a police convention in Buffalo, New York, about a Ford administration plan to increase the cost of a federal firearms license.
5. Ibid.
6. *Sorrels v. United States.*
7. John Lewis, "America's Gun Police," *Inquiry*, March 3, 1980, p. 10.
8. Ibid; the original source of this statement was a survey form sent to members and others by the Second Amendment Foundation as part of its task force investigation of BATF enforcement policies.
9. BATF director Dickerson to Senator DeConcini, September 7, 1979.
10. David Hardy, Proceedings, Second Amendment Foundation Legal Activists Conference, Boston, August 17, 1980.
11. Ibid.
12. 18 USC S923(g).
13. *Terry v. Ohio,* 392 U.S. 1 (1968).
14. *Camara v. Municipal Court,* 387 U.S. 523 (1967).
15. *U.S. v. Biswell,* 406 U.S. 311 (1972).
16. Ibid.
17. *Marshall v. Barlow,* 98 S. Ct. 1816 (1978).
18. Ibid.
19. David Hardy, transcript, *Oversight Hearings on Bureau of Alcohol, Tobacco and Firearms,* before Senate Committee on Appropriations (Washington, D.C.: U.S. Government Printing Office, 1979), p. 274.
20. John Lewis, "American Gestapo," *Reason,* April 1980, p. 28.
21. Vernon Acree, *Oversight Hearings on Bureau of Alcohol, Tobacco and Firearms,* p. 17.
22. Hardy, *War,* p. 77.
23. Ibid., p. 78.
24. Ibid., pp. 80-81.
25. John Lewis, "The Bureau of Alcohol, Tobacco and Firearms and the Second Amendment," *New Guard,* Fall 1979, p. 33.

26. *U.S. v. Brown*, 24 *Crim. Law Reporter* 2285 (S.D.N.Y. Oct. 29, 1978).
27. Ibid.
28. Ibid.
29. Hardy, *War*, p. 43.
30. Ibid., p. 89.
31. Ibid.
32. 18 USC 921. a (21).
33. 18 USC 923 (g) (1) (A).
34. 18 USC 926.

Chapter 4

Rights of Gun Owners During Arrest and Trial

*I*F THE POLICE OR BATF *arrive at my home and demand entrance to search my house for suspected illegally possessed firearms, can I deny them entrance?*

If the police have a valid search warrant, you may not offer resistance to their search and seizure of the weapons listed in their warrant. The warrant may read "John Doe" instead of your personal name; however, it must have your correct address and be signed by a judge or magistrate.

If the police lack a search warrant and ask me to consent to a search, is it prudent for me to agree?

Because an informer may have surreptitiously hidden an illegal firearm in your home, it is best that you decline the search, and ask the police to obtain a search warrant, while you phone your attorney. If you agree to the search, and planted contraband weapons are found in your house, the prosecutor will contend that the contraband is your personal property, and it will be your burden to prove otherwise.

What if the policemen force their way into my home without showing a search warrant, or ignore my rejection of a consenting search?

Loudly voice your opposition to the search, but do not offer any physical or armed resistance to the policemen. They will outnumber you, and unless you're built like Charles Atlas, you'll spend much of the following day looking in your pile carpet for your teeth. Remember, since the agents did not have a search warrant, and were not in "hot pursuit" of a criminal, the evidence they seize during the raid will not be admitted as evidence into trial by the judge.

Does BATF have the right to enter my gun shop and immediately proceed to inspect or even confiscate my sales and inventory records without a search warrant?

Yes.[1]

If I am arrested by the police for a firearms offense, what are my rights as a suspect?

Before arresting you, the police may question you about your alleged involvement in the offense. Anything you say during this questioning period may be entered as self-incriminating evidence against yourself at trial. Not until you are taken into "custody" are the police required to inform you of your Miranda rights, which are:

1. You have the right to remain silent.
2. If you give up the right to remain silent, anything you say can and will be used against you in a court of law.
3. You have the right to speak with an attorney and have him present during all questioning. If you cannot afford the services of an attorney, you may have one appointed by the court at no charge.
4. Do you understand each of these rights as I have

explained them to you? Bearing your rights in mind, do you wish to make a statement at this time?

Even before you are formally charged, you may decline answering the policemen's questions, even though they suggest that "it will be much easier for you to answer our questions here than at the station."

Why should I decline answering the policemen's questions until I obtain advice from an attorney?

Because as many states impose a mandatory jail sentence for offenses involving a firearm, it is best to remain silent until your attorney is beside you for consultation. The wisdom of this course of action can be ascertained from preliminary negotiations that have occurred between prosecutors and defense counsels in firearm-related arrests in Massachusetts. For example, let us imagine that you are an honest, noncriminal store owner in Roxbury, Massachusetts, a high-crime suburb of Boston. You have attempted to obtain a carrying-concealed-handgun permit, but the antigun police chief refuses to issue you a permit. Because you fear being robbed while leaving your shop late at night, you decide to carry a loaded concealed handgun despite the permit denial. Several nights later police officers stop you for weaving between traffic lanes. You tell them you're tired from working late; they think you're drunk. You step out of your car for a breath-analysis test; they search you and find your gun. You are arrested for carrying a concealed gun without a license. If you blurt out during arraignment at the police station, "Yes, I was carrying a concealed gun in my pocket while driving on the street," you've just talked yourself into a one-year-long jail imprisonment, for that is the mandatory penalty in Massachusetts for your offense.

However, had you the presence of mind to remain silent upon arrest and phoned your attorney, he would have informed you that he could plea-bargain with the prosecutor's office into having you plead guilty of being in illegal "possession" of a firearm, an offense whose punishment will produce a monetary fine, but not mandatory imprisonment, as there is no mandatory imprisonment sentence for gun owners caught in illegal possession of a firearm. When the prosecutor discovers that you have no criminal record, and you had attempted to obtain a carrying-concealed-handgun permit, he probably will be interested more in obtaining a quick guilty plea on the lesser charge of illegal possession than in fighting a prolonged, costly trial on the carrying charge, which the prosecutor might lose.

Once I begin to respond voluntarily to some of the questions, may I stop answering them?

Yes. The Miranda decision allows a suspect to answer only those questions which he desires to, such as name, residence, family members, and other non-self-incriminating information.

What happens to me once I have been arrested and taken to the police station?

Upon arrival you will be fingerprinted, photographed, and allowed to phone your family or attorney. The next morning, unless it is Sunday, you will be brought before a judge who will decide whether you should be released either upon your own personal recognizance or on bail, or be returned to jail until the trial.

How should I select an attorney who will best represent me?

If your family attorney cannot assist you, phone the Second Amendment Foundation's Attorney Referral Service at its hot line number: 206-454-7012. If you have been arrested in a case where you have unintentionally violated a firearm law, or are a victim of BATF harassment, or believe that your offense was not an intentional personal-assault crime (such as robbery), SAF will review its law-yer-referral files in an attempt to match you up with a sympathetic progun attorney in your community.

If I am arrested, under what circumstances am I entitled to free legal counsel?

To receive the services of a free court-appointed de-fense attorney, (1) you must be indigent and (2) your offense must be a criminal act that is punishable by an im-prisonment sentence.

How do I determine if I am poor enough to receive free legal counsel?

Shortly after your arrest, at your arraignment hearing, the judge will inquire whether you can show that you are indigent (no or little income, small savings, or negligible property ownership). If you are found to be indigent, the judge will order the Public Defender's Office to provide you with counsel, or he will contract with a local attorney to defend you at no cost to yourself.

Should I feel that I am being needlessly harassed by BATF and decide to sue it, what kind of payment arrangement can I work out with an attorney?

There are three basic agreements: (1) flat fee--a speci-fied amount for which the attorney will argue your case through a certain court, such as the trial or appellate court; (2) contingency fee--a previously agreed-upon payment once there is a successful settlement to the case; here there will be little or no payment from the client; and (3) ongoing payment--payment made until the case is settled or the client decides to drop the suit because he can no longer afford it.

Even though I am found to be indigent and thereby qualify for a court-appointed attorney, should I consider seeking other financial assistance in obtaining an attorney of my own choosing?

The adage to remember here is that you get what you pay for. Although you can ask the judge to appoint as counsel an attorney who you feel would best represent you, the judge may deny your request. A disinterested public defender will probably feel obligated to keep you from receiving the maximum penalty; however, he, or any other non-progun attorney, may be disinclined to challenge every charge that is brought against you. A disinterested attorney may decide to obtain for you the quickest plea-bargained settlement that he can. In contrast is the concerned progun attorney who is willing to challenge all the indictments. Remember, where offenses of the Gun Control Act are alleged, [2] conviction upon any one count makes the defendant a felon. Such judgments will evermore prevent you from possessing or handling firearms.[3] You will also be required to divest yourself of all your personal firearms. Thus, because of the harsh penalties that may be imposed upon you, you should consider obtaining an attorney who is philosophically inclined to your progun viewpoints and who will therefore mount a strong defense on your behalf.

If I am arrested on a firearms offense charge and my firearm is seized, will the gun be returned to me?

That depends upon state law. Some states require that firearms used in an offense be destroyed; that sometimes occurs even in cases where the defendant has been found innocent. In other states, judges not infrequently have the discretionary power to determine whether seized firearms are to be returned to their owners, or to be destroyed. In one Alaska case,[4] the judge opined that as a condition for allowing the defendant to plead guilty to a lesser charge, his handgun would be destroyed by the state without compensation to the gun owner. However, as the gun was to be used as payment for the attorney's services, the judge should give the gun to the attorney. The judge concurred with this novel appeal.

Can you recommend a book which would be very useful to me in understanding how attorney-client relationships work?

One fine legal-advice publication, which cites hundreds of legal precedent cases, and which should be read by anyone involved in any legal action, is The Rights of Lawyers and Clients, Stephen Gillers, Avon Books, The Hearst Corp., NY, NY (1979).

What are some issues that I should be concerned about while my attorney is preparing my defense case?

Following is a list of issues you should discuss with your attorney to see if they are applicable to your case:[5]

1. *Negotiation and Plea-Bargaining*
   · Can you plead and still preserve issues for appeal?
   · Do you set a bad precedent by appealing?
   · How do you read the prosecutor? Does he really intend to go to trial on this case?
   · What does the prosecution know about guns and gun laws? What do the people's likely "experts" know about the subject?
   · Voir dire: what history can you get on their experts?
   · Discovery: what weaknesses do the documents reveal?
   · Have you got all the data? Tapes, recordings, photos; have you gone over the list of prospective witnesses and jurors?
   · How does the sentence/balance swing for your client? Will he profit by the exposure that a trial will give him?

- Challenges to the court.
- Can you sell your superior knowledge of the subject matter to the prosecution? Is the prosecution afraid of your ability?
- Can the prosecution get its witnesses? Vacation schedules?

2. *Trial Technique*

- Impressions on the jury by the defendant: haircuts, clothes, attitudes.
- What is the prosecutor like?
- Does your client "sell," does he present himself well?
- Jury selection: are antigun jurors being seated?
- Education of the nonshooter, judge and juror; we have to teach them why we have firearms in our community. Justification for the sport or self-defense.
- Are progun experts available for testimonial support?
- Cross-examination of prosecution experts: do you really know more about the subject than he does? Does it show? Can you cross-examine without referring to notes?
- Getting federal witnesses into court: motions to produce or dismiss.
- Contents of the declaration for production (facts).
- Exhibits and models; testing techniques.

3. *Motions*

- Custodial status of the defendant when making incriminating statements.
- Suppression: search and seizure considerations.

4. *Civil Cases*

- Explaining to the client the different standards of proof.
- Bonds; civil forfeiture; destruction.
- Appraisals of firearm's value; challenge to the govern-

ment's appraisal.
· Motions for summary judgment (proper use of the motion).

5. *Records on Appeal*
   · Looking through the eyes of the appellate judge.
   · Reopening to put in omitted facts.
   · Findings and special findings: route to successful appeal.
   · Conclusions of law: are they appropriate here?

6. *Judgment*
   · Penalty enhancement: why did defendant have a gun?
   · Did defendant possess a firearm?
   · Did defendant use a firearm?
   · Was the firearm operable? Does it matter?

7. *Alternatives*
   · Deferred prosecution.
   · Tax counts.
   · Misdemeanors.
   · Dismissing federal prosecution in favor of state prosecution.

How might the federal Youth Corrections Act affect my felony conviction record?

Felony offenders, younger than twenty-six, who are sentenced under the YCA of 1950 (18 USC 5021) and who receive an unconditional discharge from probation or parole before the expiration of their maximum sentence, may apply to have their felony convictions "set aside." The relevance of this law to gun owners is that it enables young gun owners who have received a felony conviction (say, for violating a provision of the 1969 GCA) once again to purchase and possess firearms. The YCA was designed to prevent vulnerable young offenders from becoming habitual criminals. [6]

Notes on Chapter 4

1. 27 CFR 178.23; Treasury Dept. News Release B-1210; *U.S. v. Hatfield*, U.S. Court of Appeals, Sixth Cir. 78-5416.
2. 18 USC 924.
3. 18 USC 925(c).
4. *State of Alaska v. David Ross* (defendant), in Dist. Ct., State of Alaska, 77-636CR (May 10, 1977); *Shooting Times*, November 1980.
5. John Fell, paper presented at Second Amendment Foundation Legal Training Conference, Boston, August 17, 1980.
6. Jay Schaefer, "The Federal Youth Corrections Act: The Purposes and Uses of Vacating the Conviction," *Federal Probation*, September 1975; *William D. Weiner v. U.S. Bureau of Alcohol, Tobacco and Firearms, et al.*, 78 Civ. 3739 (E.D.N.Y.); Howard Criswell, "ATF Changes Position of Youth Corrections Act Disabilities," *BATF/Dept. of Treasury News*, December 31, 1979, FY-80-21; *U.S. v. Arrington* (CA-5: 1980).

Chapter 5

Rights of Those Using Firearms for Self-Defense

*U*NDER WHAT CIRCUMSTANCES MAY I SHOOT AN ASSAILANT?

Self-defense laws vary from state to state, but in general, a gun owner may shoot a robber, mugger, or housebreaker, only to escape imminent and unavoidable danger of death or grave bodily harm. Some states require that the victim actually attempt to retreat, and only when his back is against a wall, can he shoot his life-threatening assailant.[1]

May I shoot a person who is stripping my car?

In most states, no. A shooting is usually justifiable only when a victim's life and limb are in jeopardy. Most states even frown upon a gun owner using his firearm to discourage a vandal from fleeing, while he awaits the arrival of the police. Although it may offend a gun owner's macho, the smart thing to do is phone for police assistance--if possible. [2]

How about an individual who constantly threatens to "punch my lights out"; can I shoot him the next time he jeers at me?

No. Courts dislike your shooting someone who is only verbally insulting you. Even when he raises a fist at you, the courts would rather you retreat than draw your gun, despite your humiliation of having to back down. The assailant must attempt to strike you with deadly force before you may use your firearm to defend yourself. Even after you have pulled your firearm, and the assailant attempts to flee, you cannot shoot him in his back--as his actions are no longer jeopardizing you. Although most gun owners possess a gun for self-defense, they must understand the statutory limitations that define the circumstances in which armed self-defense is justifiable. A gun cannot be used to defend one's pride; it may be used only for defending one's life, and in a few instances, one's property. In general, "the right of self-defense begins when danger begins, ends when the danger ends, and revives when the danger returns."[3]

For what other reasons may I not use my firearms?

The defensive firearm is a protection tool, a special-purpose life-insurance policy designed to deep one alive. it doesn't cover vengeance, theft, insult, vandalism, or vigilante justice. Only the immediate threat of death or severe injury should remove the civilian's gun from its holster or drawer; and once that threat confronts, no other instrument or strategy so effectively ensures the survival of the innocent.[4]

When do I have the right to make a "citizen's arrest"?

Generally, only when a civilian witnesses a felony. And only in those rare circumstances when an assailant is threatening others with grave bodily harm or possible death should a gun owner use his firearm to stop the felony from occurring or expanding.[5]

What is a felony?

A felony is a criminal act punishable by death or imprisonment for more than one year.[6] Felonious acts include homicide, arson, rape, robbery, mayhem, burglary, and larceny. However, as burglary and larceny are crimes rather against property than against the person, and seldom threaten the property owner's life or limb, many states do not allow their citizens to use firearms to capture such a felon. It may prove disadvantageous for a gun owner to attempt to do so.

A case in point. Residents of New York State are required to obtain a firearm-possession permit from the police before they purchase a pistol. However, suppose the police deny the permit request and an applicant decides surreptitiously to obtain a pistol. Suppose further that the applicant, on hearing a crime victim cry for assistance, rushes gun in hand to arrest the assailant. You may suppose still further that the gun owner has done himself no favor. For when New York police officers arrive to take the mugger into custody, they will also arrest the gun owner for illegal possession and illegal carrying of a pistol. The mugger will receive an imprisonment of several months if he has a serious criminal history; otherwise he will not be sent to jail. However, the brave gun owner, upon conviction for illegal carrying, will be imprisoned for at least one year because that is New York's mandatory penalty for that offense. So much for justice in the Empire State.

Thus, the gun owner must know his state, county, and city gun-control laws, comply with them, and understand in what circumstances he may use his firearm for self-defense.

Attesting this is the sad experience of New York City resident Jack Weingarten. Hearing noises at night outside near his car, Weingarten observed several youths attempting illegally to enter his car. Weingarten and his son reached for their rifles and attempted to capture the suspects for the police. During the ensuing melee, Jack fired two warning shots into the air, and captured one suspect, while the other one fled. Upon arrival, the police officers released on the spot the prisoner, due to lack of supporting evidence that he was attempting to break into Weingarten's car. However, as the police had gone to the trouble of driving to the scene of a reported crime, they arrested Weingarten and his son for carrying firearms illegally outside their home without a carrying license, as well as for firing a gun within city limits. Though they had licenses to possess the rifles inside their home, they had failed to obtain a firearm-carrying license for carrying loaded guns outside their residence. Fortunately, Weingarten contacted a sympathetic progun attorney, who was able to plea-bargain the original charges down to the lower offense of disorderly conduct. Both were fined $25, but the fact that neither was convicted of a crime prevented his firearm-possession permit from being automatically and permanently revoked.

Are whistles and tear-gas sprays more effective means of self-defense for women than a handgun?

Definitely not. Any male assailant can quickly knock away a whistle that a woman is blowing. And there are several disadvantages in using mace or other tear-gas devices against assailants: (1) most cities forbid their citizens to possess or carry them; (2) most of the devices on the civilian market are ineffective because they contain chemicals weak enough to be sold in communities that curtail the use of stronger maces; and (3) most assailants will not hesitate to knock away the canister because they know it is ineffective unless sprayed directly into their eyes. The aerosol sprays are actually worse than nothing at all, because they lull women into a false sense of security.

What for women are the advantages of a handgun over, say, knives or karate?

The gun is quickly learned. It is manageable. It is certain power. The woman doesn't have to join the Green

Berets to learn how to defend herself properly with a knife. Nor does she have to spend several months learning a few rudimentary karate stances, which will undoubtedly be ineffective against a determined assailant. Why this, and more, when within a few minutes a person can learn to load, aim, and fire a pistol? Of course, any gun owner should occasionally practice target shooting in order to become more confident in using a gun during those nervous moments of being victimized. A handgun can be quickly drawn and requires little practice so it can be effectively used for self-defense.

What's the best handgun for a woman to carry?

The smaller calibers do not have enough stopping power, and some of the larger calibers have a severe recoil. A fair compromise for the novice shooter (of any sex) is the .38 revolver, which has adequate stopping power and a moderate recoil.[7]

How effective is handgun self-defense?

An analysis of the various means of self-defense (handgun, fist fighting, running away, or shouting) used against robbers disclosed that the single most effective means of thwarting a robbery was the handgun, as reported to Chicago police during 1975.[8]

When I see an individual running from the scene of a crime, may I shoot at the suspect?

No, because unless you saw that individual actually assault the victim, you might be shooting an individual who is running to summon help, or who may be a co-victim in pursuit of the assailant.

If I witness a felonious crime against a victim, may I use my gun to go to his aid?

Such assistance is permissible in many states, in certain circumstances. A 1965 case in Illinois established the general criteria of when a gun owner may assist a victim who is being threatened with deadly assault:

> (1) that force is threatened against a person; (2) that the person threatened is not the aggressor; (3) that the danger of harm is imminent; (4) that the force threatened is unlawful; (5) that the person threatened must actually believe; (a) that a danger exists, (b) that the use of force is necessary to avert the danger, (c) that the kind and amount of force which he uses are necessary; and (6) that the above beliefs are reasonable. There is a further principle involved when the defendant uses deadly force [in] those situations in which (a) the threatened force will cause death or great bodily harm or (b) the force threatened is a forcible felony. [9]

In sum, the gun owner must remember that the only time he may use his firearms for self-defense is when he or a victim is attempting to escape imminent and unavoidable danger of death or grave bodily harm. Infrequently, state codes specify when a gun owner may use his firearm to prevent the theft of property. The wise gun owner will visit his local library to review his state's criminal codes to determine when he may lawfully discharge his firearm for valid self-defense purposes.

After I have watched the neighborhood kids or their pets trample across my front lawn for the umpteenth time after I have warned them not to do so, may I wave my gun at them to scare them off?

No. The kid's parents will complain to the police department, which most certainly will charge you with any of the following offenses: reckless endangerment, assault, disturbing the peace, disorderly conduct; and should you fire a "warning shot" into the air, you will be charged for violating the city ordinance that prohibits discharging firearms within city limits. The gun exists to protect your life, not your well-manicured lawn.

Notes on Chapter 5

1. Massad F. Ayoob, *In the Gravest Extreme: The Role of the Firearm in Personal Protection* (1979) (Box 122, Concord, N.H.), pp. 10-14.
2. Ibid.
3. Ibid.
4. Massad F. Ayoob, *Armed and Alive* (Bellevue, Wash.: Second Amendment Foundation, 1980), p. 6.
5. Ayoob, *Gravest Extreme*, p. 27.
6. 18 USC 1.
7. Conversation with *Women & Guns* editor Sonny Jones.
8. *The Saturday Night Special: Why It Should Not Be Banned* (Bellevue, Wash.: Second Amendment Foundation, 1978), pp. 7-8.
9. James B. Whisker, *Our Vanishing Freedom: The Right to Keep and Bear Arms* (McLean, Va.: Heritage House Publications, 1972), pp. 31-49.

Chapter 6

Federal Firearms Regulations

*W*HAT FEDERAL LEGISLATION REGULATES THE SALE OF FIREARMS?

There have been five such laws: the National Firearms Act (1934), the Federal Firearms Act (1938), the Omnibus Crime Control and Safe Streets Act (1968), the Gun Control Act (1968), and the Firearms Owners' Protection Act (1986).

What regulatory impact does the National Firearms Act (NFA) have upon ownership?

The NFA (enacted June 26, 1934) is a tax law rather than a regulatory law, and its constitutionality has been upheld repeatedly.[1] Because the act's sponsors were worried that the Supreme Court might declare that Congress did not have the constitutional authority to regulate the sale of certain firearms, this bill was disguised as a new tax law, which is an issue that can be regulated by Congress.

The NFA (which is still law as 26 USC 4181-4191):

1. Makes it a federal offense for anyone to possess certain extraordinarily dangerous weapons, such as machine-guns, rifles, shotguns whose barrels are less than eighteen inches in length, and silencers, unless their owner has a federal permit to possess such weapons. Those arms are to be registered with the Department of Treasury (BATF) and a $200 transfer tax per weapon is paid by the buyer; 2. Requires all firearm manufacturers, importers, and dealers to pay a registration fee to the Department of Treasury; 3. Orders all firearm manufacturers and importers to stamp an identification serial number upon all their firearms, and makes it unlawful for anyone to alter those

marks; 4. Requires all firearm manufacturers, importers, and dealers to keep records of their sales.

What was the impact of the Federal Firearms Act (FFA)?

Federal control in regulating the commerce in and possession of firearms. It: 1. Required all manufacturers, dealers, and importers of firearms, ammunition, and components to register and obtain a federal firearms license from the Department of Treasury (BATF); 2. Stipulated that all licensed manufacturers, importers, and dealers must maintain importation and sales records of their firearms and ammunition; 3. Forbade individuals indicted or convicted of a crime of violence from shipping or receiving any firearm in interstate commerce; 4. Made it unlawful for anyone to possess any firearm whose serial number had been obliterated or altered; 5. Forbade anyone from possessing ammunition or firearms that had been stolen during interstate transportation.

Although individuals "engaged in the business of selling firearms or ammunition" were required to obtain a dealer's license, any other civilian could travel to another state to purchase any firearm (if that transaction did not violate state or local law), or order any firearm through the mail. These liberties were curtailed by two acts, the Omnibus Crime Act and the Gun Control Act.

What is the significance of the Omnibus Crime Control and Safe Streets Act?

The Crime Act (enacted June 19, 1968) repealed the 1938 Federal Firearms Act after having incorporated significant portions of the earlier act. The major new codes (which are still in effect as 18 USC 921; 2510 and 42 USC 3701) are: 1. Licensed gun dealers may not sell handguns to out-of-state residents, except to other licensed dealers; 2. A non-licensee may not travel to another state to buy firearms, except rifles or shotguns; 3. No person may sell or transfer any firearms other than rifles or shotguns to an out-of-state individual; 4. A person must be twenty-one years of age before he may purchase a handgun; 5. Importation of firearms is unlawful, except under certain conditions; 6. Firearms made before 1899 are exempted from regulation by this act; 7. Possession of a firearm with the intent of using it to commit an offense is an unlawful act and may be punished with the maximum penalty of a $10,000 fine or a ten-year imprisonment, or both; 8. Individuals who are dishonorably discharged from the military, or have renounced their citizenship, or are illegal aliens, or are adjudged mental incompetents, may not receive, transport, or possess any firearm.

Provisions of the 1938 Federal Firearms Act which are retained (and are still law) are: 1. Firearm manufacturers and dealers must be federally licensed; 2. Felons, fugitives, and indicted persons may not possess firearms; 3. Serial numbers of firearms may not be altered; 4. Manufacturers and dealers must keep records of their disposed firearms.

How did the Gun Control Act amend the earlier federal firearm codes?

The GCA (enacted October 22, 1968) amended Chapter 44 of 18 USC (a provision of Title IV of the Omnibus Crime Act) by substituting the contents of Title I of the GCA, which are: 1. Importers, as well as manufacturers and dealers, must have a federal license to be "engaged in the business" of dealing in firearms; 2. All mail-order sales of firearms and ammunition are prohibited, except between licensed dealers; 3. "Form 4473" must be used by dealers to record the buyer, and those records must be kept for inspection by the police. The buyer must sign the form's statement that he: is not a fugitive; has not been dishonorably discharged from the military; is not unlawfully using drugs; has not been committed to a mental institution; has not otherwise been forbidden by state or local law from possessing firearms; 4. Certain small, foreign handguns are prohibited from being imported; however, their parts are not restricted from being imported; 5. Dealers may not sell firearms or ammunition to anyone under eighteen, or handguns to anyone under twenty-one years of age; 6. Any firearm used or intended to be used in any violation of the GCA is subject to seizure and forfeiture; 7. Any social offender may seek "relief from disability" from the Secretary of the Treasury and thereby be eligible to possess firearms, except individuals who have violated the GCA, such as a criminal who used a firearm to commit a crime, or even an otherwise law-abiding gun owner who innocently violated the GCA; 8. Anyone who carries a firearm with the intent of using it to commit any federal felony shall be sentenced to an imprisonment of not less than one year and not more than ten years; 9. Any firearm manufactured before 1899 is exempted from the regulations of this act; 10. A collector's license is necessary for those individuals who collect certain, dangerous, or "curio" weapons, which non-licensed civilians cannot possess; 11. A month-long "amnesty" period is granted individuals possessing illegal weapons so that they can register them with the Treasury Department and thereby retain possession of those weapons; 12. Anyone who intends to commit an offense punishable by imprisonment exceeding one year, and ships or receives a firearm or ammunition, is subject to a fine of up to $10,000 or ten years' imprisonment, or both; 13. A person may not sell a firearm to anyone who lives in another state, unless the buyer is a dealer; 14. Only dealers may sell rifles or shotguns to out-of-state residents if both states permit such sales, and the states are contiguous.

How did the 1986 Firearms Owners' Protection Act affect the 1968 Gun Control Act?

There were changes made to eight sections of Title I of The Gun Control Act of 1968. The definitions section was changed by adding the language "engaged in the business of" in place of "manufacture of." The Unlawful Acts section was changed by the removal of ammunition sales and the addition of classes of individuals not allowed to purchase guns. New possession and transfer of machine-guns also became illegal. The Licensing section was changed to allow collectors to dispose of personal collections without a license and make dealers' record-keeping requirements stricter. The penalties section was changed to increase the penalties for crimes committed with a gun. The Exceptions section was changed by removing some discretion from the Secretary of the Treasury and directing the Secretary to allow the importation of weapons for scientific purposes. The Rules & Regulations section prohibited the establishment of a firearms registration system. A new section was added to allow gun owners to transport their weapons through gun banning areas without prosecution. Finally, stricter penalties were put in place for the use of restricted ammunition in the commission of a crime.

Are there any other federal laws that seriously affect firearm sales?

The Mutual Security Act of 1954 (22 RSC 1934) authorizes the President to regulate the import and export of firearms. Regulations that have been issued under this act require persons engaged in the importation and exportation of munitions to register with the Treasury Department and maintain disposition records.

Other interrelated acts that concern the sales and development of war machinery are the Arms Control and Disarmament Act of 1961 (amended 1977), the Arms Export Control Act of 1961 (amended 1977), and the Arms Export Control Act of 1968 (22 USC 2551, 2567, 2751).

QUESTIONS AND ANSWERS ABOUT FEDERAL GUN CONTROL LAWS

The following series of questions and answers clarify federal gun-control laws. Although federal codes may permit certain firearm transactions, such acts may be forbidden by state law. The reader must therefore remember that any of the following answers may be altered by state law. Thus, before the reader follows these interpretations, he must determine how his actions may be impeded or prohibited by his state, county, or city gun control ordinances. Although local ordinances may impose firearm regulations that are more restrictive than those required by federal law, they cannot reduce the federal minimum standards.

The following answers were derived from the gun control standards enacted by the National Firearms Act of 1934 (26 USC 4181-4191) and the Gun Control Act of 1968 (18 USC 921-928). The Codes of Federal Regulations (27 CFR 178-179) have been researched for additional clarification of the federal firearm laws.

I. GENERAL

Must gun merchants be licensed?
Yes. Manufacturers, importers, exporters, and dealers of firearms must obtain various Federal Firearm Licenses (FFL) to engage in their line of business.[2]

Are antique firearms regulated by the GCA?
Not those manufactured before 1899, or their modern reproductions, so long as they are not designed or redesigned to use rimfire or centerfire fixed ammunition.[3]

Is ammunition regulated?
Ammunition is defined at 178.11 (CFR27), but

records need to be kept for armor piercing ammunition only.[4]

Is the sale of firearm parts regulated by the GCA?
Aside from mufflers and silencers, only the receivers or frames are regulated, as they are regarded as complete firearms.[5]

II. GUN-SELLING LICENSE (FFL)

Whom do I contact to obtain a Federal Firearms License (FFL)?
Request your local BATF office (see Appendix C) to send to you its ATF Form 7, which is an application to become a firearms dealer.

Once I have my FFL, at which locations may I sell my firearms?
The FFL enables you to sell firearms at only one location: the site you request, the selling address of which is listed on the FFL. However, you may apply for additional FFLs for the other locations where you want to sell firearms.[6]

May a licensed dealer sell his guns at a gun show?
No. He may display his firearms at the show and take orders, but he must return his firearms to his store, record the transaction, and then transfer the firearm to its buyer.[7]

III. NON-FFL INDIVIDUALS

Under what circumstances may a non-licensed civilian sell a firearm?
A civilian (depending also upon state law) may buy or sell only within the state in which he legally resides; but he may sell a firearm to any FFL dealer in any other state, and he may buy a rifle or shotgun from an FFL dealer

in a contiguous state when both the buyer's and seller's states permit such sales.[8]

May I sell my personal firearms to out-of-state persons?

No. Such transfers are unlawful, unless they are sold to an FFL dealer.[9]

May I sell personal firearms to someone who lives in my state?

Yes. There is nothing in the Gun Control Act which prohibits such a sale between residents of the same state provided the sale is not in violation of state or local ordinances and the purchaser is not prohibited by any provision of the GCA from acquiring or possessing a firearm. In general, a single sale, unattended by other circumstances, does not require that a person be licensed.[10]

May I buy ammunition in another state and bring it back to my home state?

Yes, but it must be for personal use. A licensed dealer may ship ammunition out of state only to another dealer.[11]

Who may not receive or possess firearms?

Title I of the Gun Control Act prohibits the following individuals from shipping or receiving firearms or ammunition: (a) those under indictment or convicted of a crime punishable by more than a year's imprisonment; (b) those who are fugitives from justice; (c) those who have been adjudged mentally defective or committed to a mental institution; and (d) those who use or are addicted to marijuana or narcotics. Title VII of the Omnibus Crime Control and Safe Streets Act prohibits the following individuals from receiving, possessing or transporting a firearm in or affecting commerce: (a) convicted felons; (b) those discharged from the military under dishonorable conditions; (c) those adjudged mentally incompetent; (d) those who have renounced their American Citizenship; and (e) unlawful aliens in America.[12]

How may a felon possess firearms?

Any felon convicted of a crime punishable by imprisonment for a term exceeding one year (except for a crime committed with a firearm or other weapon, or for a violation of the Gun Control Act or the National Firearms Act) may apply to the Secretary of the Treasury for "relief from disabilities" imposed by federal firearm laws. Approval of such relief would allow a felon to purchase and possess firearms.[13]

Does a federal permit exist that would allow me to carry firearms while I am vacationing or undertaking a business trip through other states?

No. Some states have a mandatory jail-imprisonment law whereby civilians who do not possess a state-issued firearm-carrying permit and are convicted of, for example, merely having an unloaded firearm in their car trunk, will be automatically imprisoned for a year even if they committed no other crime. If you plan to take a firearm into another state, telephone that state's highway patrol to learn how you can legally transport a firearm through that state.

May firearms be shipped through the mail?

Civilians may mail rifles and shotguns. Only licensed dealers and licensed collectors may mail handguns. All such mailings must comply with U.S. postal regulations in the 124.4 Postal Service Manual.

May I take my firearms when I move to another state?

Only if the state to which you are moving allows it. As your new state or city of residence may have special licensing or registration laws, check with the city police to see if such transfers are permissible. Transfer of certain

GCA Title II or NFA firearms[14] must be approved by the Secretary of the Treasury before transfer. If a carrier is hired to do the moving, he must be notified that firearms are in the shipment.[15]

How may a civilian purchase a firearm from another non-licensed civilian who resides in a different state?

Such a transaction can be made when the buyer requests his local FFL dealer to order the firearm from the out-of-state seller.[16]

How may foreign visitors purchase firearms?

After a legal alien has resided within a state for at least ninety days he may purchase firearms, if state or city laws do not forbid such purchases. He can make a purchase sooner if he has written permission from his country's consulate. The letter is valid for purchasing firearms only within the state that is the residence of both the foreigner and his consulate.[17]

IV. FIREARMS TRANSACTION RECORD: FORMS

When non-licensed civilians sell personal firearms, do they need to field Form 4473?

No. Only FFL licensees are required to file that form.[18]

When a dealer decides to purchase a firearm from his store's inventory, does he need to record that sale?

Yes. The dealer must use Form 4473 to record the transaction.[19]

May a social-security card be used to identify a buyer?

No, because valid ID must contain the buyer's birth date and address, both of which must be evident to the licensed seller.[20]

When must Form 4473 be signed?

It is to be signed when the dealer physically transfers the firearm to the person who signed the form.[21]

V. FFL DEALERS: REQUIRED RECORDS

Are dealers required to maintain records of their sales?

Yes. Besides keeping Form 4473, they must permanently maintain ledgers listing their sales. Separate ledgers are to list ammunition sales from firearm sales, and the dealer may elect to have ledgers for handguns separate from those for rifle or shotgun sales. The ledgers, however, which may be loose-leaf pages, must be consecutively numbered, and record the sales in an orderly manner. The procedures governing the recording of acquisitions and disposals are explained in 27 CFR 178.125.

Do record-keeping controls exist for rented firearms?

Yes. Licensed gun shops or pawnshops must require individuals who are renting firearms for lawful sporting purposes to execute Form 4473, upon which the renter states it is not unlawful for him to possess a firearm. This form does not need to be executed by individuals who are in temporary possession of the borrowed firearm while firing on the premises of sport or hunting clubs.[22]

VI. DEALER CONDUCT

Do federal licensees need to comply with state or local gun-control ordinances?

Yes. The GCA makes it unlawful for licensed manufacturers, importers, dealers, or collectors to make firearm transactions which are in violation of any state law or local ordinance.[23]

What is a "contiguous state" firearm sale?

The sale, by a dealer, of a rifle or shotgun to a

resident of a state that borders the dealer's state and that has enacted legislation permitting such a transaction.[24]

May a dealer make a firearm sale to out-of-state residents?

Usually not, unless (a) a bordering state has enacted a contiguous-state firearm-buying law; (b) the rifle or shotgun buyer gives a sworn statement that his rifle or shotgun was lost or stolen while he was in the state participating in a firing match or on a hunting trip; or (c) the buyer requests that his purchase be shipped to a licensed dealer within his state who can legally transfer the firearm to the buyer.[25]

Must ammunition sales be signed for by the buyer?

Although the seller is required to have the ammunition buyer show proper identification so that the seller can record the buyer's name, address, and date of birth, federal law does not require the buyer to sign for his receipt of the ammunition, except for armor piercing ammunition; state or local law, however, might impose that requirement.[26]

How old must one be to purchase firearms?

Buyers must be eighteen years of age before they may purchase rifles or shotguns or ammunition for those firearms. Handguns and handgun ammunition may be sold to those twenty-one years of age or older. Even when states allow such sales to younger individuals, dealers must comply with state law when it imposes older ages for firearm buyers. Federal law is not violated when a parent gives a firearm to his underage children, unless a child has a criminal record; has been adjudged mentally incompetent or been placed in a mental institution; has been addicted to narcotics; or has committed an offense that prohibits him from possessing firearms.[27]

VII. GUN SHOWS

May firearms and ammunition be sold at a gun show?

According to the BATF publication "Federal Regulation of Firearms and Ammunition," certain restricted sales may be made at gun shows.

A licensed firearms dealer may: (1) Display and take orders for firearms and ammunition. Orders must be filled only at the dealer's licensed premises; (2) Buy firearms from and ammunition from a licensed collector and any non-licensee (178.50 and 178.94). A non-licensed resident of the state in which the show is being held may: (1) Make an occasional sale of a firearm to another non-licensee residing in his state (as long as he is not "engaging in the business"); (2) Buy firearms from a non-licensee residing in his state. A licensed collector may: (1) Buy curios and relics from any source; (2) Dispose of curios and relics to another licensed collector or to non-licensee residents in his state.[28]

VIII. COLLECTORS

What is a collector's license?

A license that permits civilians to obtain firearms or ammunition of special interest to collectors by reason of some quality not ordinarily associated with firearms intended for sporting use or for offensive or defensive purposes. A list of such items is available from your local BATF office. The license permits one to order curio- and relic- designated firearms through the mail from any out-of-state source, and to dispose of such firearms to any other licensed collector or to non-licensed residents in one's state. However, if a collector acquires curios or relics to resell rather than to enhance a collection, the collector is required to obtain an FFL dealer's license. Even with that license, a collector of National Firearms Act firearms needs to pay the special (occupational) tax prescribed by the NFA.[29]

Do civilians need a collector's license to buy curio and relic firearms?

No. The benefit of the license is that it permits one to purchase and sell curios and relics in interstate and foreign commerce.[30]

How would a dealer benefit by obtaining a collector's license?

Since a dealer's license allows a dealer to sell his firearm and ammunition inventory (including curios and relics) only at his gun shop, a collector's license would authorize a dealer to sell his curio and relic firearms at gun shows or other locations to another licensed collector or to non-licensed residents in his state.[31]

IX. MANUFACTURERS

Do I need a license to manufacture a rifle, handgun, or shotgun?

No, as long as it is not a firearm regulated by the NFA, or one to be sold or distributed.[32]

Is a manufacturer's license needed for those who reload ammunition?

The reloader does if he sells or "distributes" the reloads, but not if he manufactures them solely for his own use.[33]

X. GUNSMITHS

Do I need a license when I engrave, repair, refinish, or customize a firearm?

Such work is considered proper to a gunsmith and a license needs to be obtained.[34]

XI. PAWNBROKERS

Does a pawnbroker need to execute a Form 4473 when he returns a firearm to the individual who pawned it?

Yes. Even though the gun owner surrenders his claim ticket to the pawnbroker, the pawnbroker must require the gun owner to complete Form 4473, just as if the transaction were a regular firearm sale. The pawnbroker must also record the transaction, and maintain a permanent sales record, like any other gun dealer. Furthermore, the firearm may be returned or sold only to an individual legally eligible to purchase a firearm. Thus, a teenager can pawn a handgun, but he must be at least twenty-one years of age before the pawnbroker can return the handgun to him. Nor can any other prohibited person pawn a firearm and later seek to have it returned. A pawnbroker must follow the same firearm sales requirements that are imposed upon regular FFL dealers, for a dealer Federal Firearms License and a firearm pawnshop dealer FFL are one and the same. An FFL pawnbroker may purchase firearms from a manufacturer in preference to merely selling the guns that are pawned to him.[35]

May anyone redeem a firearm?

A pawnbroker may not return a pawned firearm to a person prohibited from purchasing firearms. Handguns may not be returned to individuals under the age of twenty-one, nor to out-of-state pawners. Long arms may be returned to those who are at least eighteen and who live in-state or in a contiguous state. A prohibited person may not recover a pawned firearm.[36]

XII. IMPORTS AND EXPORTS

May a civilian import a firearm?

No. Individuals may obtain foreign firearms at a local gun shop, which orders them through a licensed firearms import dealer when the local dealer doesn't have a firearms import license.[37]

May personal firearms be exported?
Firearm export sales are regulated by the Arms Export Control Act of 1976, which stipulates that such transactions must be cleared by the Office of Munitions Control, U.S. Department of State, Washington, D.C. The export of sporting shotguns is regulated by the Office of Export Administration, U.S. Department of Commerce, Washington, D.C.

XIII. NATIONAL FIREARMS ACT WEAPONS
(26 USC 4181-4191, 5801-5872)

What kinds of firearms are illegal to possess unless they are registered in accordance with the National Firearms Act?
The following firearms may not be possessed by civilians without permission from BATF: machine-guns, silencers, bazookas, sawed-off shotguns or rifles, and any other NFA weapon, such as pen guns and cane guns.[38]

How may civilians acquire NFA firearms?
Civilians may submit BATF Form 4 to the director of BATF, who then decides whether or not to grant permission to the applicant to procure the weapon. A $200 (registration) transfer tax must be paid each time a weapon is transferred to a new buyer, though only a $5 tax is imposed upon "any other" classified NFA weapon.[39]

Do I need a license to sell NFA weapons?
Yes. Besides obtaining a regular Federal Firearms License, an NFA dealer must pay an annual $500 special (occupational) tax.[40]

Who determines what an NFA weapon is?
The NFA itself defines what weapons are to be

taxed (regulated) by the act. The director of the BATF may decide that certain NFA weapons may be classified as a collector's curio and relic item, that is, one unlikely to be used as a criminal weapon. Such classifications are exempted from the $200 transfer tax but are still regulated by the curio and relic provisions of the Gun Control Act.[41]

If I discover an unregistered NFA weapon, how can I register it?
　　　Such cannot be done because all unregistered NFA weapons had to be registered by the end of November 1968, and all such weapons legally manufactured since then have been automatically registered. Thus, recent discoveries of unregistered NFA weapons are unlawful to possess.[42]

What are the penalties if I am caught possessing an unregistered NFA weapon?
　　　Violators can be fined as much as $10,000 or be imprisoned up to ten years, or both, as well as have civil penalties and property forfeitures imposed upon them.[43]

May overseas servicemen bring home souvenir firearms?
　　　Soldiers may submit BATF Form 6 to the Director of BATF; the Director may then issue a permit authorizing the importation of firearms or ammunition into the United States to the place of residence of any military member of the U.S. armed forces who is on active duty outside the U.S., or who has been on active duty outside the U.S. within a sixty-day period immediately preceding the intended importation — provided that such firearms or ammunition is generally recognized as suitable for sporting purposes. Furthermore, firearms determined by the Department of Defense to be war souvenirs may be imported by military personnel under such procedures as the Department of Defense may issue.[44]

XIV. MISCELLANEOUS

How may I ship firearms through the mail?

Handguns and other firearms capable of being concealed upon the person (rifles with barrels under sixteen inches or shotguns with barrels under eighteen inches) may not be shipped through U.S. post office. Excluded from this prohibition are certain military officers, police officers, federal officers, and shipments between licensed gun dealers and manufacturers; however, those individuals must file shipment affidavits with the post office, and have them approved, before mailing.[45]

If I can't mail my firearm, how else may I ship it?

The United Parcel Service (UPS) will ship handguns and long arms, which are in need of repair, from a gun owner to a licensed gunsmith or manufacturer, and then return it to the gun owner. Remember, though, it is a violation of the GCA for a gun owner to sell or transfer a firearm to an out-of-state civilian who is not a licensed gun dealer or manufacturer.[46]

May I carry firearms into national parks?

Firearms may not be taken into "natural and historical areas and national parks," unless they are unloaded and cased or otherwise packed in such a way as to prevent their use while in the park areas. Exceptions are licensed guides, who may obtain a National Park Service permit to carry a firearm, and policemen on official business, who may pack their firearms. Civilians may carry a firearm into certain "recreational areas" of a national park; however, they should inquire with the park superintendent as to where those sites are located.[47]

Under what circumstances may a firearm be taken aboard an airplane?

A civilian may not carry openly or concealed a

loaded or unloaded firearm or other dangerous weapon or explosive on his person or in his carry-on baggage into any commercial aircraft.[48] Passengers may pack only unloaded firearms into their checked baggage, which will be stored in the hold.[49]

If I have a gubernatorial pardon, will this automatically expunge my criminal record and thereby enable me to possess firearms?

No. Even though an ex-felon has received a gubernatorial pardon, several courts have decided[50] that he, when attempting to purchase a firearm, must declare to a gun dealer that he has a prior felony conviction. The rub here is that once a felon has made that statement to a dealer, the GCA makes it illegal for the dealer to sell or transfer a firearm to the ex-felon. The GCA also makes it illegal for a convicted felon to fail to inform a gun dealer that he has a felony conviction. Felons who desire to purchase or possess firearms may seek a "relief from disabilities" decision from BATF; an approving decision would enable them to possess firearms.

What effect does a presidential pardon have upon my felony conviction?

A pardon granted by the President of the United States regarding a conviction for a crime punishable by imprisonment for a term exceeding one year removes any disability that otherwise would be imposed by the provisions of the GCA or the Omnibus Crime Control and Safe Streets Act.[51] The relevance of a presidential pardon is that it restores to gun owners convicted of being "engaged in the business of dealing in firearms" without a Federal Firearms License (such as those who sold portions of their firearms collections), the right to procure firearms legally.

Can the Secretary of the Treasury establish an "amnesty period" during which illegally possessed NFA weapons (machine-guns, etc.) may be registered with the BATF without penalties being levied upon their owner?

Yes. Such was originally done in November 1968, shortly after the enactment of the GCA. "The Secretary of the Treasury, after publication in the Federal Register of his intention to do so, is authorized to establish such period of amnesty, not to exceed ninety days in the case of any single period, and immunity from liability during any such period..."[52]

May gun owners who have received a felony conviction for violating the GCA possess black-powder or rimfire-ammunition firearms?

That question is answered by a BATF memo:

A felon's receipt, shipment, or transportation of such a firearm is not prohibited by Title I of the Gun Control Act (18 USC Chapter 44) since it is exempt from regulation as an "antique firearm." That term is defined in 18 USC 921(a) (16) as any firearm manufactured in or before 1898 and certain replicas of antique firearms made after 1898. However, it is our opinion that Title IV of the Omnibus Crime Control and Safe Street Act of 1968 (18 USC App. 1201-1203) would prohibit a felon's possession of rimfire-ammunition handguns regardless of their date of manufacture. It should be noted that Title VII contains no express exemption for antique firearms. Rather, its definitions of handgun, shotgun, and rifle include only those weapons designed to use fixed ammunition. Firearms employing antique ignition systems are not within the scope of Title VII. Consequently, while a felon may lawfully receive or possess antique-ignition-system firearms, he is precluded from lawful receipt or possession of rimfire-ammunition firearms.[53]

Notes on Chapter 6

1. *U.S. v. Freed* (1971) 401 US 601, 91 SCt 1112; *U.S. v. Oa* (1971) 448 F2d 892, cert den (1972) 405 US 935, 92 SCt 979; *Lauchil v. U.S.*, CA7 1973, 481 F2d 408,   cert den (1973) 414 US 1065, 94 SCt 571.
2. 18 USC 923; CFR 178.47.
3. 18 USC 921 (a)(11).
4. 27 CFR 178.11 and 178.125(c).
5. 27 CFR 178.11.
6. 27 CFR 178.50.
7. 27 CFR 178.50.
8. 27 CFR 178.30; 178.96.
9. 27 CFR 178.30.
10. "Federal Regulation of Firearms and Ammunition." BATF P 5300.12 (10/   79); 27 CFR 179.42.
11. 18 USC 922(a)(2).
12. 27 CFR 178.32.
13. 18 USC 925(c).
14. 27 CFR 178.28.
15. 27 CFR 178.31.
16. 27 CFR 178.29.
17. 27 CFR 178.11.
18. 27 CFR 178.124.
19. 27 CFR 178.124.
20. 27 CFR 178.124(c).
21. 27 CFR 178.124(f).
22. 27 CFR 178.97; 178.124(e).
23. 18 USC 922(b)(2).
24. 27 CFR 178.96(c); 178.124(f).
25. 27 CFR 178.96.
26. 27 CFR 178.125(c).
27. 27 CFR 178.99.
28. 178.50; 178.93.
29. 27 CFR 178.11 curios; 178.41(c)(d); 178.50; 178.93.
30. 27 CFR 178.41(c); 178.50.
31. 27 CFR 178.50; 178.93.
32. 27 CFR 178.41.
33. 27 CFR 178.41.
34. 27 CFR 178.11 — dealer.
35. 27 CFR 178.99; 178.124; 178.125.
36. 18 USC 922(a)(2).
37. 27 CFR 178.113; 27 CFR 47; 27 CFR 178-179.
38. 27 CFR 179.
39. 27 CFR 179.82; 179.84.

40. 27 CFR 179.31; 179.34.

41. 27 CFR 179.11; 179.24; 179.25.

42. 27 CFR 179.101(b).

43. 27 CFR 179.181; 179.182.

44. 27 CFR 178.114.

45. 18 USC 1715-1716; Post Office "Domestic Mail Manual," 124.4.

46. 27 CFR 2.11.

47. 36 CFR 2.11.

48. Federal Aviation Act, 14 USC 1472(L).

49. 14 CFR 121.585.

50. *U.S. v. Matassini*, CA-5 1978, 565 F2d 1297; *Thrall v. Wolfe*, CA-7 1974, 503 F2d 313, cert den (1975) 420 US 972, 95 SCt 1392.

51. 27 CFR 178.142; 18 USC 1203.

52. 26 USC 5801(d); 18 USC 926.

53. BATF assistant director Miles Keathley to SAF research director Bill Garrison, August 22, 1980.

Chapter 7

State and Local Gun Control Ordinances

CAN STATES IMPOSE GUN CONTROLS *that are more restrictive than federal controls?*

Yes. Federal laws establish minimum standards that state laws cannot negate. For example, states cannot enact legislation that would permit sixteen-year olds to purchase handguns, because the federal minimum age is twenty-one years. However, cities can and have imposed local handgun sale codes that are more restrictive than federal laws, such as the Morton Grove, Illinois, ordinance that prohibits handguns within city limits.

Do state constitutions protect an individual's right to possess firearms?

Most states have constitutional provisions that clearly guarantee the individual's right to possess firearms; some states are silent on the issue. Besides the firearm-possession clauses, many state codes detail in what circumstances individuals have the right to use deadly force in defending themselves and family against certain life-threatening assailants. Those codes are outlined at the end of this chapter. A note of caution: new laws are passed all the time and those codes could have changed.

What is a firearm-registration law?

Such laws can be enacted by cities as well as by states. They usually require a gun owner to register his gun's serial number, along with his name and address, with the state, county, or city police. Those laws also usually require a gun owner to notify the police of those to whom he has recently sold one of his registered firearms.

How does gun-owner licensing differ from firearm registration?
Licensing requires a gun owner to obtain either a firearm-purchase or firearm-possession permit before he may procure a firearm. Those licenses are issued after the police department has determined that the applicant doesn't have a criminal record, which would bar him from possessing firearms. However, in some areas, such as in New York City, the issuance of a license may be infrequent, as anti-gun politicians attempt to deprive the citizens of self-defense firearms. It has not been statistically proven that licensing or registration laws keep criminals from obtaining firearms, or deter criminal activity. Some licenses indicate that they are valid only for specific locations; a home gun permit, for instance, entitles a gun owner to keep a gun at home, but he has to obtain a store gun permit if he wants to carry a gun while working at his store.

What is a carrying-concealed-weapons (handgun) permit?
A carrying-concealed-weapons permit usually allows an individual to carry a concealed handgun upon himself while away from home. However, states may impose restrictions that sharply curtail the carrying privilege. The permit may be valid only while the permittee is commuting directly between his home and business; only within the county or city the permittee resides in; or be applicable state-wide. Permittees must also check their state law to determine if their concealed gun must be carried upon their person at all times or if it may be temporarily stored beneath the driver's seat or in the glove box. Arizona and Texas, for instance, prohibit civilians from carrying concealed handguns entirely.

Do I need a carrying-concealed-handgun permit if I place a loaded handgun either on the passengers seat or on the dashboard?

State laws vary on answering this issue. Some prohibit the carrying of any loaded firearm in your car if it is not on your person; others stipulate that a gun must be unloaded and stored in the trunk of the car while its ammo is secured in the glove box. Because of the wide variances in these laws, visit your local police station to review your city, county, and state gun-control laws.

How do cooling-off or waiting periods affect my obtaining firearms?

These periods have two supposed benefits: (1) preventing jilted lovers from immediately purchasing a firearm to terminate their ex-'s, and (2) allowing police officers time to check their files to determine if the buyer has a history that would preclude him from possessing a firearm. The effectiveness of these waiting periods, however, is questionable in all of the states having them; a three-day waiting period is too short for the police to conduct a profile search, and California police departments have learned that even their state's fifteen-day waiting period isn't long enough for conducting an effective investigation. Some state attorneys general have opined that these waiting periods apply to civilian firearm sales as well as gun shop sales. Furthermore, a three-day waiting period could mean: (a) that a gun dealer could allow a buyer to pick up his firearm three days after paying for it, or (b) that the police must be given three working days to conduct a check before the transfer could occur. The difficultly with the waiting-period policy is that it prevents civilians from quickly obtaining self-defense firearms whenever the police strike or city riots develop. Recognizing this, several states have shunned a cooling-off period even for handgun sales.

May a police chief refuse to issue me a gun-possession or a carrying-concealed-weapon permit?

Again, that depends upon state law. In Washington State a police department is required by law to issue a carrying-concealed-weapons permit thirty days after it was applied for, even if the police have had insufficient time to do a character check on the applicant. In some other states, the county sheriff has the discretionary power in determining whether a carrying-concealed-weapon permit is to be issued. The result is that some sheriffs approve virtually all noncriminal applicants, whereas others issue only a handful of permits.

Even though state law may allow me to carry a handgun openly in a holster on the outside of my clothing without my obtaining a carrying-concealed-handgun permit, can a city require me to obtain that permit if I carry the holstered handgun inside city limits, or even ban the gun?

Yes. In Arizona, state law allows citizens to carry unconcealed handguns, but in Tombstone, all guns must be checked in and left with the town marshal. Furthermore, even though state law may permit the carrying of guns in a holster, an anti-gun police chief might order his patrolmen to arrest citizens who openly carry firearms, on the trumped-up charge of disturbing the peace. Such arrests have been made previously, and anti-gun judges have occasionally convicted the gun carriers.

The following list outlines the gun-possession laws of each state, and should prove helpful to gun owners who wish to carry firearms interstate.

Alabama

Constitutional guarantee: That every citizen has a right to bear arms in defense of himself and the state. [Art. 1, sec. 26]

Self-defense code: Kittrell v. State, 291 Ala. 156, 279 So.2d 426 (1973). Wall v. State, 49 Ala.App.285, 270 So.2d 831 (1972). VanderWielen v. State, 47 Ala.App.108, 251 So.2nd 240 (1971).

		Code No.
Carrying Concealed Weapons (firearm) permit available?	Yes	13-6-155
Open holster-gun carrying permissible without license?	No[1]	13-6-120(II)
Firearm-possession permit required to possess gun at home?	No	13-6-153
Firearm-possession permit required to possess gun at work?	No	13-6-153
Gun owner's identification card or firearm-purchase-approval permit required before a resident may buy a handgun?	No[2]	13A-11-77
Are firearms required to be registered with state police or similar firearms-registration bureau?	No[3]	13A-11-77
Waiting period after handgun purchase?	2 days	

1. Limited.
2. Handgun buyers at gun shops are required to complete a handgun-approval form, which is submitted for approval to the local police department.
3. Gun shops required to keep registers on individuals buying handguns.

Alaska
Constitutional guarantee: A well-regulated militia being necessary to the security of a free state, the right of the people to keep and bear arms shall not be infringed [Art 1,

sec. 19]
Self-defense code: 11.81.335-.400 (see also 11.61.200) Justification: Uses of deadly force in defense of self, (a) use deadly force upon another person when and to the extent (1) the use of non-deadly force is justified under sec. 330 of this chapter; and (2) the person reasonably believes the use of deadly force is necessary to defend himself from death, serious physical injury, kidnapping, sexual assault in the first degree under AS 11.41.410(a)(1) or (2), sexual assault in the second degree, or robbery in any degree. (b) A person may not use deadly force under this section if he knows that he can with complete safety as to himself and others avoid the necessity of so doing by retreating, except there is no duty to retreat if the person is (1) on premises which he owns or which are leased to him and he is not the initial aggressor; or (2) a peace officer acting within the scope and authority of his employment or a person assisting a peace officer under sec.380 of this chapter.

		Code No.
Carrying Concealed Weapons (firearm) permit available?	No[1]	11.61.200
Open holster-gun carrying permissible without license?	Yes[2]	11.62.200
Firearm-possession permit required to possess gun at home?	No	
Firearm-possession permit required to possess gun at work?	No	
Gun owner's identification card or firearm-purchase-approval permit required before a resident may buy a handgun?	No	
Are firearms required to be registered with state police or similar firearms-	No	

registration bureau?

Waiting period after   No
handgun purchase?

1. Illegal to carry guns concealed, except on private property when personal protection is required during such activities as hunting or cross country skiing.

2. Except in bars or where liquor is served.

NOTE As city or county gun-control codes may be more restrictive than state law, inquire of your local police about how local codes affect your possession and use of firearms.

Arizona

Constitutional guarantee: The right of the individual citizen to bear arms in defense of himself or the state shall not be impaired, but nothing in this section shall be construed as authorizing individuals or corporations to organize, maintain, or employ an armed body of men. [Art. 2, sec. 26]

		Code No.
Carrying Concealed Weapons (firearm) permit available?	No[1]	13-3102
Open holster-gun carrying permissible without license?	Yes[2]	13-3102(E)
Firearm-possession permit required to possess gun at home?	No	
Firearm-possession permit required to possess gun at work?	No	
Gun owner's identification card or firearm-purchase-approval permit required before a resident may buy a handgun?	No	
Are firearms required to be registered with state police or similar firearms-	No	

registration bureau?
Waiting period after   None
handgun purchase?
1. Civilians may not carry handguns concealed.
2. Except Tombstone.
NOTE: As city or county gun-control codes may be more restrictive than state law, inquire of your local police about how local codes affect your possession and use of firearms.

Arkansas
Constitutional guarantee:The citizens of this state shall have the right to keep and bear arms for their common defense.[Art. 2, sec .5]

		Code No.
Carrying Concealed Weapons (firearm) permit available?	No[1]	41-3101
Open holster-gun carrying permissible without license?	No[1]	41-3101
Firearm-possession permit required to possess gun at home?	No	
Firearm-possession permit required to possess gun at work?	No	
Gun owner's identification card or firearm-purchase-approval permit required before a resident may buy a handgun?	No	
Are firearms required to be registered with state police or similar firearms-registration bureau?	No	
Waiting period after handgun purchase?	None	

1. It is illegal for an individual to carry firearms "on or about his person, in a vehicle occupied by him, or other-

wise readily available for use with a purpose to employ it as a weapon against a person."

NOTE: As city or county gun-control codes may be more restrictive than state law, inquire of your local police about how local codes affect your possession and use of firearms.

California

Constitutional guarantee: None. See Penal Code 12021-12026 and Government Code 53071

Self-defense code: Penal Code 197

Homicide is justifiable when committed by any person in any of the following cases: 1. When resisting any attempt to murder any person, or to commit a felony, or to do some great bodily injury upon any person; or, 2. When committed in defense of habitation, property, or person, against one who manifestly intends or endeavors, by violence or surprise, to commit a felony, or against one who manifestly intends and endeavors, in a violent, riotous or tumultuous manner, to enter the habitation of another for the purpose of offering violence to any person therein; or, 3. When committed in the lawful defense of such person ... when there is reasonable ground to apprehend a design to commit a felony or to do some great bodily injury, and imminent danger of such design being accomplished; but such person, or the person in whose behalf the defense was made, if he was the assailant or engaged in mutual combat, must really and in good faith have endeavored to decline any further struggle before the homicide was committed; or, 4. When necessarily committed in attempting, by lawful ways and means, to apprehend any person for any felony committed, or in lawfully suppressing any riot, or in lawfully keeping and preserving the peace.

		Code No.
Carrying Concealed Weapons (firearm) permit available?	Yes	12025/12050
Open holster-gun carrying permissible without license?	Yes[1]	12025(c)

Firearm-possession permit required to possess gun at home?	No[2]	12026
Firearm-possession permit required to possess gun at work?	No	12026
Gun owner's identification card or firearm-purchase-approval permit required before a resident may buy a handgun?	No	12076
Are firearms required to be registered with state police or similar firearms-registration bureau?	No[2]	
Waiting period after handgun purchase?	15 days[3]	

1. Legal, but highly inadvisable. You will be arrested for disturbing the peace, according to the San Diego Police.
2. Permit required for possession of certain semi-automatics.
3. All firearms.
NOTE: As city or county gun-control codes may be more restrictive than state law, inquire of your local police about how local codes affect your possession and use of firearms.

Colorado
Constitutional guarantee: The right of no person to keep and bear arms in defense of his home, person and property, or in aid of the civil power when thereto legally summoned, shall be called in question; but nothing herein contained shall be construed to justify the practice of carrying concealed weapons.
Self-defense code: 18-1-704
(1) Except as provided in subsections (2) and (3) of this section, a person is justified in using physical force upon another person in order to defend himself or a third person

from what he reasonably believes to be the use or imminent use of unlawful physical force by that person, and he may use a degree of force which he reasonably believes to be necessary for that purpose. (2) Deadly physical force may be used only if a person reasonably believes a lesser degree of force is inadequate and: (a) The actor has reasonable ground to believe, and does believe, that he or another person is in imminent danger of being killed or of receiving great bodily harm; or (b) The other person is using or reasonably appears about to use physical force against an occupant of a dwelling or business establishment while committing or attempting to commit burglary...[or kidnapping, or sexual assault (18-3-4), or assault (18-3-202/203)—Ed..]

		Code No.
Carrying Concealed Weapons (firearm) permit available?	Yes[2]	18-12-105
Open holster-gun carrying permissible without license?	Yes	18-12-105
Firearm-possession permit required to possess gun at home?	No	
Firearm-possession permit required to possess gun at work?	No	
Gun owner's identification card or firearm-purchase-approval permit required before a resident may buy a handgun?	No	
Are firearms required to be registered with state police or similar firearms-registration bureau?	No[1]	
Waiting period after handgun purchase?	None	

1. Gunshops are to record those who purchase a handgun, but not report such sales.
2. Restrictive issuance. Dependent upon county.
NOTE: As city or county gun-control codes may be more restrictive than state law, inquire of your local police about how local codes affect your possession and use of firearms.

Connecticut

Constitutional guarantee: Every citizen has a right to bear arms in defense of himself and the state.[Art. 1, sec. 15]
Self-defense code: See State Code Title 53: Homicide.

		Code No.
Carrying Concealed Weapons (firearm) permit available?	Yes	53-202
Open holster-gun carrying permissible without license?	No	29-28
Firearm-possession permit required to possess gun at home?	No	
Firearm-possession permit required to possess gun at work?	No	
Gun owner's identification card or firearm-purchase-approval permit required before a resident may buy a handgun?	Yes	29-33
Are firearms required to be registered with state police or similar firearms-registration bureau?	Yes[1]	29-33
Waiting period after handgun purchase?	14 days[2]	

1. Handguns only.
2. None with CCW permit.
NOTE: As city or county gun-control codes may be more

restrictive than state law, inquire of your local police about how local codes affect your possession and use of firearms.

Delaware
Constitutional guarantee: none
Self-defense code:

		Code No.
Carrying Concealed Weapons (firearm) permit available?	Yes	11-1441
Open holster-gun carrying permissible without license?	No	11-1441
Firearm-possession permit required to possess gun at home?	No	
Firearm-possession permit required to possess gun at work?	No	
Gun owner's identification card or firearm-purchase-approval permit required before a resident may buy a handgun?	No	
Are firearms required to be registered with state police or similar firearms-registration bureau?	No	
Waiting period after handgun purchase?	None	

See a; sp 11-222; 24-902; 28-801
NOTE: As city or county gun-control codes may be more restrictive than state law, inquire of your local police about how local codes affect you possession and use of firearms.

Florida
Constitutional guarantee: The right of the people to keep and bear arms in defense of themselves and of the lawful

authority of the state shall not be infringed, except that manner of bearing arms may be regulated by law.[Art. 1, sec. 8]

Self-defense code: 782.02

The use of deadly force is justifiable when a person is resisting any attempt to murder such person or to commit any felony upon him or upon or in any dwelling house in which such person shall be.

		Code No.
Carrying Concealed Weapons (firearm) permit available?	Yes	790.05; 790.06
Open holster-gun carrying permissible without license?	Yes	790.06
Firearm-possession permit required to possess gun at home?	No	790.25(3)(n)
Firearm-possession permit required to possess gun at work?	No	790.25(3)(n)
Gun owner's identification card or firearm-purchase-approval permit required before a resident may buy a handgun?	No	
Are firearms required to be registered with state police or similar firearms-registration bureau?	Yes[1]	
Waiting period after handgun purchase?	3 days	

1. Gun shops report handgun sales to local police.

See *Ensor v. State*, 403 So.349 (FLA 1981)

NOTE: As city or county gun-control codes may be more restrictive than state law, inquire of your local police about how local codes affect your possession and use of firearms.

Georgia

Constitutional guarantee: The right of the people to keep and bear arms, shall not be infringed, but the General Assembly shall have power to prescribe the manner in which arms may be borne. (Art. 1.1, par. 22]

Self-defense code:

		Code No.
Carrying Concealed Weapons (firearm) permit available?	Yes	26-2904
Open holster-gun carrying permissible without license?	No	26-2904
Firearm-possession permit required to possess gun at home?	No	
Firearm-possession permit required to possess gun at work?	No	
Gun owner's identification card or firearm-purchase-approval permit required before a resident may buy a handgun?	No	
Are firearms required to be registered with state police or similar firearms-registration bureau?	No	
Waiting period after handgun purchase?	None	

NOTE: As city or county gun-control codes may be more restrictive than state law, inquire of your local police about how local codes affect your possession and use of firearms.

Hawaii

Constitutional Guarantee: A well-regulated militia being necessary to the security of a free state, the right of the

people to keep and bear arms shall not be infringed. [Art. 1, sec. 15]
Self-defense code:

		Code No.
Carrying Concealed Weapons (firearm) permit available?	Yes	134-9
Open holster-gun carrying permissible without license?	No	134-9
Firearm-possession permit required to possess gun at home?	Yes	134-3
Firearm-possession permit required to possess gun at work?	Yes	134-3
Gun owner's identification card or firearm-purchase-approval permit required before a resident may buy a handgun?	Yes	134-3(a)
Are firearms required to be registered with state police or similar firearms-registration bureau?	Yes	134-2
Waiting period after handgun purchase?	15 days	134-3(h)

NOTE: As city or county gun-control codes may be more restrictive than state law, inquire of your local police about how local codes affect your possession and use of firearms.

Idaho
Constitutional guarantee: The people have the right to keep and bear arms, which right shall not be abridged; but this provision shall not prevent the passage of laws to govern the carrying of weapons concealed on the person, nor prevent passage of legislation providing minimum

sentences for crimes committed while in possession of a firearm, nor prevent the passage of legislation providing penalties for the possession of firearms by a convicted felon, (nor prevent the passage of any legislation punishing the use of a firearm). No law shall impose licensor, registration, or special taxation on the ownership or possession of firearms or ammunition. Nor shall any law permit the confiscation of firearm, except those actually used in the commission of a felony. [Art. 1, sec. II]

Self-defense code: 18-4009; 18-4010; 19-201; 19-202.

Homicide is also justifiable when committed by any person in either of the following cases: 1. when resisting any attempt to murder any person, or to commit a felony, or to do some great bodily injury upon any person; or, 2. when committed in defense of habitation, property, or person, against one who manifestly intends or endeavors, by violence or surprise, to commit a felony, or against one who manifestly intends and endeavors in a violent, riotous, or tumultuous manner, to enter the habitation of another for the purpose of offering violence to any person therein; or, 3. when committed in the lawful defense of such person...[or family member] ... when there is reasonable ground to apprehend a design to commit a felony or to do some great bodily injury, and imminent danger of such design being accomplished; but such person, or the person in whose behalf the defense was made, if he was the assailant or engaged in mortal combat, must really in good faith have endeavored to decline any further struggle before the homicide was committed; or 4. when necessarily committed in attempting, by lawful ways and means, to apprehend any person for any felony committed, or in lawfully suppressing any riot, or in lawfully keeping and preserving the peace.

		Code No.
Carrying Concealed Weapons (firearm) permit available?	Yes	18-3302

Open holster-gun carrying permissible without license?	Yes[1]	18-3302
Firearm-possession permit required to possess gun at home?	No	
Firearm-possession permit required to possess gun at work?	No	
Gun owner's identification card or firearm-purchase-approval permit required before a resident may buy a handgun?	No	
Are firearms required to be registered with state police or similar firearms-registration bureau?	No	
Waiting period after handgun purchase?	None	

1. Only while hunting.

NOTE: As city or county gun-control codes may be more restrictive than stat law, inquire of your local police about how local codes affect your possession and use of firearms.

Illinois

Constitutional guarantee: Subject only to the police power, the right of the individual citizen to keep and bear arms shall not be infringed. [Art. 1, sec. 22]
Self-defense code: 38-7 (1-14)

		Code No.
Carrying Concealed Weapons (firearm) permit available?	No[5]	38-24-1(a)(4)
Open holster-gun carrying permissible without license?	Yes[1]	38-24-1
Firearm-possession permit required to possess gun at home?	Yes[2]	38-24-1(a)(10)

Firearm-possession permit required to possess gun at work?	Yes[3]	
Gun owner's identification card or firearm-purchase-approval permit required before a resident may buy a handgun?	Yes	83-2(a)
Are firearms required to be registered with state police or similar firearms-registration bureau?	No	
Waiting period after handgun purchase?	3 days	38-24-3

1. But must be unloaded in city or municipality. Banned in most cities.

2. Firearm owner's I.D. card.

3. Firearm owner's I.D. card.

4. Long arms: 24 hours.

5. May carry concealed at one's home, land, or place of business.

NOTE: As city or county gun-control codes may be more restrictive than state law, inquire of your local police about how local codes affect your possession and use of firearms. Some cities have a total ban on the possession of handguns.

Indiana

Constitutional guarantee: The people shall have a right to bear arms, for the defense of themselves and the state. [Art. 1, sec. 32]

Self-defense code: 35-41-3-2.

(a) A person is justified in using reasonable force against another person to protect himself or a third person from what he reasonably believes to be imminent use of unlawful force. However, a person is justified in using deadly force only if he reasonably believes that force is necessary to prevent serious bodily injury to himself or a third person or the commission of a forcible felony.

(b) A person is justified in using reasonable force, including deadly force, against another person if he reasonably believes that the force is necessary to prevent or terminate the other persons unlawful entry of or attack on his dwelling or curtilage...(35-41-3-2)

		Code No.
Carrying Concealed Weapons (firearm) permit available?	Yes	35-23-4.1-5
Open holster-gun carrying permissible without license?	No[1]	35-23-4.1-3
Firearm-possession permit required to possess gun at home?	No	35-23-4.1-3
Firearm-possession permit required to possess gun at work?	No	35-23-4.1-3
Gun owner's identification card or firearm-purchase-approval permit required before a resident may buy a handgun?	Yes[2]	35-47-2-8
Are firearms required to be registered with state police or similar firearms-registration bureau?	Yes[3]	35-23-4.1-7(d)
Waiting period after handgun purchase?	7 days[4]	35-47-2-8(c)

1. Permissible on one's own property or fixed place of business.
2. Application to transfer a handgun.
3. Private transactions must be reported by dealer.
4. Waived for any person to whom a handgun-carrying license has been issued; handgun sales reported to police.
NOTE: As city or county gun-control codes may be more

restrictive than state law, inquire of your local police about how local codes affect your possession and use of firearms.

Iowa
Constitutional guarantee: none
Self-defense code: 704.

Reasonable force is that force which a reasonable person, in like circumstances, would judge to be necessary to prevent an injury or loss, and no more, except that the use of deadly force against another is reasonable only to resist a like force or threat.

		Code No.
Carrying Concealed Weapons (firearm) permit available?	Yes	724.4(8)
Open holster-gun carrying permissible without license?	Yes[1]	724.4
Firearm-possession permit required to possess gun at home?	No	724.4(1)
Firearm-possession permit required to possess gun at work?	No	724.4(1)
Gun owner's identification card or firearm-purchase-approval permit required before a resident may buy a handgun?	Yes[2]	724.15-.20
Are firearms required to be registered with state police or similar firearms-registration bureau?	No	
Waiting period after handgun purchase?	None	724.20

1. Permissible outside of city limits, but not in car.
2. Permit valid for one year.

NOTE: As city or county gun-control codes may be more restrictive than state law, inquire of your local police about how local codes affect your possession and use of firearms.

Kansas
Constitutional guarantee: The people have the right to bear arms for their defense and security; but standing armies, in time of peace, are dangerous to liberty, and shall not be tolerated, and the military shall be in strict subordination to civil power. [Art. 1, sec. 4]
Self-defense code:

		Code No.
Carrying Concealed Weapons (firearm) permit available?	No[1]	21-4201
Open holster-gun carrying permissible without license?	Yes	21-4201
Firearm-possession permit required to possess gun at home?	No	21-4201(d)
Firearm-possession permit required to possess gun at work?	No	21-4201(d)
Gun owner's identification card or firearm-purchase-approval permit required before a resident may buy a handgun?	No	
Are firearms required to be registered with state police or similar firearms-registration bureau?	No	
Waiting period after handgun purchase?	No	

1. Illegal to carry concealed off one's property, please read this code.
NOTE: As city or county gun-control codes may be more restrictive than state law, inquire of your local police about how local codes affect your possession and use of firearms.

Kentucky

Constitutional guarantee: All men are, by nature, free and equal, and have certain inherent and inalienable rights, among which may be reckoned ... 7. The right to bear arms in defense of themselves and of the state, subject to the power of general assembly to enact laws to prevent persons from carrying concealed weapons. [Art. 1, sec. 1]

Self-defense code:

		Code No.
Carrying Concealed Weapons (firearm) permit available?	No	527.020
Open holster-gun carrying permissible without license?	Yes[1]	
Firearm-possession permit required to possess gun at home?	No	
Firearm-possession permit required to possess gun at work?	No	
Gun owner's identification card or firearm-purchase-approval permit required before a resident may buy a handgun?	No	
Are firearms required to be registered with state police or similar firearms-registration bureau?	Yes[2]	
Waiting period after handgun purchase?	None	

1. 298 Ky 800, SW (2d) 101, *Reid v. Com.*
2. Handgun sales are to be reported to city police.

NOTE: As city or county gun-control codes may be more restrictive than state law, inquire of your local police about how local codes affect your possession and use of firearms.

Louisiana

Constitutional guarantee: The right of each citizen to keep and bear arms shall not be abridged, but this provision shall not prevent the passage of laws to prohibit the carrying of weapons concealed on the person. [Art. 1, sec. 11]

Self-defense code: LRS 14:20.

A homicide is justifiable ... when committed in self-defense by one who reasonably believes that he is in imminent danger of losing life or receiving great bodily harm and that the killing is necessary to save himself from the danger.

		Code No.
Carrying Concealed Weapons (firearm) permit available?	Yes	LRS
Open holster-gun carrying permissible without license?	Yes	40:95
Firearm-possession permit required to possess gun at home?	No	
Firearm-possession permit required to possess gun at work?	No	40:1781
Gun owner's identification card or firearm-purchase-approval permit required before a resident may buy a handgun?	No	40:1783
Are firearms required to be registered with state police or similar firearms-registration bureau?	No	
Waiting period after handgun purchase?	None	

NOTE: As city or county gun-control codes may be more restrictive than state law, inquire of your local police about how local codes affect your possession and use of firearms.

Maine

Constitutional guarantee: Every citizen has a right to keep and bear arms for the common defense; and his right shall never be questioned. [Art. 1, sec. 16]

Self-defense code: 17-A 108, Maine Criminal Codes.

2. A person is justified in using deadly force upon another person: A. When he reasonably believes it necessary and he reasonably believes it such other person is: (1) About to use unlawful, deadly force against himself or a 3rd person; or (2) Committing or about to commit a kidnapping, robbery...; or B. When he reasonably believes: (1) that such other person has entered or is attempting to enter a dwelling place or has surreptitiously remained within a dwelling place without a license or privilege to do so; and (2) That deadly force is necessary to prevent the infliction of bodily injury by such other person upon himself or a 3rd person present in the dwelling place; C. However, a person is not justified in using deadly force ... if: (3) He knows that he or a 3rd person can with complete safety (a) retreat from the encounter, except, that he or the 3rd person is not required to retreat if he or the 3rd person is in his dwelling place and was not the initial aggressor...

		Code No.
Carrying Concealed Weapons (firearm) permit available?	Yes	25-2031
Open holster-gun carrying permissible without license?	Yes	25-2031
Firearm-possession permit required to possess gun at home?	No	
Firearm-possession permit required to possess gun at work?	No	
Gun owner's identification card or firearm-purchase-approval permit required before a resident may buy	No	15:15-393

a handgun?

Are firearms required to be registered with state police or similar firearms-registration bureau?	No
Waiting period after handgun purchase?	3 days

NOTE: As city or county gun-control codes may be more restrictive than state law, inquire of your local police about how local codes affect your possession and use of firearms.

Maryland[1]
Constitutional guarantee: none
Self-defense code:

		Code No.
Carrying Concealed Weapons (firearm) permit available?	Yes	27-36E
Open holster-gun carrying permissible without license?	Yes	27-36B
Firearm-possession permit required to possess gun at home?	No	27-36B(c)(3)
Firearm-possession permit required to possess gun at work?	No	27-36B(c)(3)
Gun owner's identification card or firearm-purchase-approval permit required before a resident may buy a handgun?	No	27-442
Are firearms required to be registered with state police or similar firearms-registration bureau?	Yes[2]	27-442(i)
Waiting period after handgun purchase?	7 days	27-422(b)

1. Maryland has a poor-quality handgun ban, which completely outlaws six guns. The state police and gun dealers have a list of banned guns.
2. Handgun sales only.
NOTE: As city or county gun-control codes may be more restrictive than state law, inquire of your local police about how local codes affect your possession and use of firearms.

Massachusetts
Constitutional guarantee: The people have a right to keep and bear arms for the common defense. [Part 1, art. 17]
Self-defense code: See General laws Chpt. 278 (a) [Chpt. 696 of 1981 Acts].

		Code No.
Carrying Concealed Weapons (firearm) permit available?	Yes	140-131
Open holster-gun carrying permissible without license?	No	269-10(a)
Firearm-possession permit required to possess gun at home?	Yes	140-129B
Firearm-possession permit required to possess gun at work?	Yes	140-129B
Gun owner's identification card or firearm-purchase-approval permit required before a resident may buy a handgun?	Yes	140-129B-D
Are firearms required to be registered with state police or similar firearms-registration bureau?	Yes[1]	140-128A
Waiting period after handgun purchase?	None	

1. All firearm-ownership transfers must be reported to state Commissioner of Public Safety.

NOTE: As city or county gun-control codes may be more restrictive than state law, inquire of your local police about how local codes affect your possession and use of firearms.

Michigan
Constitutional guarantee: Every person has a right to keep and bear arms for the defense of himself and the state. [Art. 1, sec. 6]
Self-defense code:

		Code No.
Carrying Concealed Weapons (firearm) permit available?	Yes	28.424
Open holster-gun carrying permissible without license?	No	28.424
Firearm-possession permit required to possess gun at home?	No	28.424
Firearm-possession permit required to possess gun at work?	No	28.424
Gun owner's identification card or firearm-purchase-approval permit required before a resident may buy a handgun?	Yes[1]	28.92
Are firearms required to be registered with state police or similar firearms-registration bureau?	No[2]	28.429
Waiting period after handgun purchase?	10 days[3]	

1. Includes sales between civilians.
2. Handgun sales to be registered at gunshops.
3. Must buy handgun within 10 days of issuance of permit.
NOTE: As city or county gun-control codes may be more restrictive than state law, inquire of your local police about

how local codes affect your possession and use of firearms.

Minnesota
Constitutional guarantee: none
Self-defense code:

		Code No.
Carrying Concealed Weapons (firearm) permit available?	Yes	624.71
Open holster-gun carrying permissible without license?	No	624.71
Firearm-possession permit required to possess gun at home?	No	
Firearm-possession permit required to possess gun at work?	No	
Gun owner's identification card or firearm-purchase-approval permit required before a resident may buy a handgun?	Yes[1]	624.7131
Are firearms required to be registered with state police or similar firearms-registration bureau?	Yes[2]	624.00
Waiting period after handgun purchase?	7 days	624.7132(4)

1. Handgun buyers must obtain permission from local police before purchase.
2. Bureau of Criminal Apprehension.
Also see: 609:66
NOTE: As city or county gun-control codes may be more restrictive than state law, inquire of your local police about how local codes affect your possession and use of firearms.

Mississippi

Constitutional guarantee: The right of every citizen to keep and bear arms in defense of his home, person, or property, or in aid of the civil power when thereto legally summoned, shall not be called in question, but the legislature may regulate or forbid carrying of concealed weapons. [Art. 3, sec. 12]

Self-defense code: 97-3-15.

The killing of a human being by the act, procurement, or commission of another shall be justifiable in the following cases: (e) when committed by any person in resisting any attempt unlawfully to kill such person or to commit any felony upon him, or upon or in any dwelling-house in which such person shall be; (f) When committed in the lawful defense of one's own person or any other human being, where there shall be reasonable ground to apprehend a design to commit a felony or to do some great personal injury, and there shall be reasonable ground to apprehend a design to commit a felony or to do some great personal injury, and there shall be imminent danger of such design being accomplished; (g) When necessarily committed in attempting by lawful ways and means to apprehend any person for any felony committed; (h) When necessarily committed in lawfully suppressing any riot or in lawfully keeping and preserving the peace.

		Code No.
Carrying Concealed Weapons (firearm) permit available?	Yes[1]	97-37-7
Open holster-gun carrying permissible without license?	No	97-37-1
Firearm-possession permit required to possess gun at home?	No	
Firearm-possession permit required to possess gun at work?	No	

Gun owner's identification card or firearm-purchase-approval permit required before a resident may buy a handgun?	No	
Are firearms required to be registered with state police or similar firearms-registration bureau?	Yes[2]	45-9-1
Waiting period after handgun purchase?	None	

1. Limited to security guards, individuals carrying valuables.

2. Handguns registered with county sheriff 10 days after purchase.

NOTE: As city or county gun-control codes may be more restrictive than state law, inquire of your local police about how local codes affect your possession and use of firearms.

Missouri

Constitutional guarantee: The right of every citizen to keep and bear arms in defense of his home, person and property, or when lawfully summoned in aid of the civil power, shall not be questioned; but this shall not justify the wearing of concealed weapons. [Art. 1, sec. 23]

Self-defense code: 563:031.

1. A person may ... use physical force upon another person when and to the extent he reasonably believes such to be necessary to defend himself or a third person from what he reasonably believes to be the use or imminent use of unlawful force by such other person,... 2. A person may not use deadly force upon another person under the circumstances specified in subsection 1 unless he reasonably believes that such deadly force is necessary to protect himself or another against death, serious physical injury, rape, sodomy, or kidnapping... 4. The defendant shall have

the burden of injecting the issue of justification under this section.

		Code No.
Carrying Concealed Weapons (firearm) permit available?	No	407.500
Open holster-gun carrying permissible without license?	Yes	407.500
Firearm-possession permit required to possess gun at home?	No	
Firearm-possession permit required to possess gun at work?	No	
Gun owner's identification card or firearm-purchase-approval permit required before a resident may buy a handgun?	Yes	571.090
Are firearms required to be registered with state police or similar firearms-registration bureau?	Yes[1]	571.090
Waiting period after handgun purchase?	7 days	571.090.3

1. With county sheriff

NOTE: As city or county gun-control codes may be more restrictive than state law, inquire of your local police about how local codes affect your possession and use of firearms.

Montana

Constitutional guarantee: The right of any person to keep and bear arms in defense of his own home, person, and property, or in aid of the civil power when thereto legally summoned, shall not be called in question, but nothing herein contained shall be held to permit the carrying of concealed weapons. [Art. 2, sec. 12]

Self-defense code:

		Code No.
Carrying Concealed Weapons (firearm) permit available?	Yes	45-8-319
Open holster-gun carrying permissible without license?	Yes	45-8-319
Firearm-possession permit required to possess gun at home?	No	45-8-317(7)
Firearm-possession permit required to possess gun at work?	No	45-8-317(7)
Gun owner's identification card or firearm-purchase-approval permit required before a resident may buy a handgun?	No	
Are firearms required to be registered with state police or similar firearms-registration bureau?	No	
Waiting period after handgun purchase?	None	

NOTE: As city or county gun-control codes may be more restrictive than state law, inquire of your local police about how local codes affect your possession and use of firearms.

Nebraska

Constitutional guarantee: "... the right to bear arms for security or defense, of self, family, home, and others, and for lawful common defense, hunting, recreational use, and all other lawful purposes, and such rights shall not be denied or infringed by the state or any subdivision thereof."

Self-defense code:

		Code No.
Carrying Concealed Weapons (firearm) permit available?	No[1]	28-1202

Open holster-gun carrying permissible without license?	No	28-1201
Firearm-possession permit required to possess gun at home?	No	28-1201
Firearm-possession permit required to possess gun at work?	No	
Gun owner's identification card or firearm-purchase-approval permit required before a resident may buy a handgun?	No	
Are firearms required to be registered with state police or similar firearms-registration bureau?	No	
Waiting period after handgun purchase?	None	

1. Neither handguns nor long arms may be carried concealed.

NOTE: As city or county gun-control codes may be more restrictive than state law, inquire of your local police about how local codes affect your possession and use of firearms.

Nevada

Constitutional guarantee: "Every citizen has the right to keep and bear arms for security and defense, for lawful hunting and recreational use and for other lawful purposes." [Art. 1, sec. 11]

Self-defense code: 200.120 et seq.

Justifiable homicide is the killing of a human being in necessary self-defense, or in defense of habitation, property, or person, against one who manifestly intends, or endeavors, by violence or surprise, to commit a felony, or against any person or persons who manifestly intend and endeavor, in a violent, riotous, or tumultuous manner, to enter the habitation of another for the purpose of assaulting or offering personal violence to any person dwelling or being therein.

		Code No.
Carrying Concealed Weapons (firearm) permit available?	Yes	202.350(4)
Open holster-gun carrying permissible without license?	Yes	202.350
Firearm-possession permit required to possess gun at home?	No[1]	
Firearm-possession permit required to possess gun at work?		
Gun owner's identification card or firearm-purchase-approval permit required before a resident may buy a handgun?	No[2]	
Are firearms required to be registered with state police or similar firearms-registration bureau?	Yes[3]	
Waiting period after handgun purchase?	None	

1. Individuals moving to Nevada must register their handguns with local police within 24 hours of arrival.
2. For first purchase only.
3. Handgun sales are to be reported to local police.
NOTE: As city or county gun-control codes may be more restrictive than state law, inquire of your local police about how local codes affect your possession and use of firearms.

New Hampshire
Constitutional guarantee: "All persons have the right to keep and bear arms in defense of themselves, their fami-

lies, their property, and the state." [Art. 2(a)]
Self-defense code:

		Code No.
Carrying Concealed Weapons (firearm) permit available?	Yes	159:6
Open holster-gun carrying permissible without license?	Yes	159:6
Firearm-possession permit required to possess gun at home?	No	159:4
Firearm-possession permit required to possess gun at work?	No	159:4
Gun owner's identification card or firearm-purchase-approval permit required before a resident may buy a handgun?	No[1]	159:8-9
Are firearms required to be registered with state police or similar firearms-registration bureau?	Yes[2]	159:9
Waiting period after handgun purchase?	None	

1. Non residents require a permit to purchase.
2. Handgun sales are to be reported to local police by dealer.
NOTE: As city or county gun-control codes may be more restrictive than state law, inquire of your local police about how local codes affect your possession and use of firearms.

New Jersey
Constitutional guarantee: none
Self-defense code: *State v. Bonano*, 59NJ 515, 284 A.2d 345 (1971).

		Code No.
Carrying Concealed Weapons (firearm) permit available?	Yes[1]	2C:39/58
Open holster-gun carrying permissible without license?	No	2C:39/58
Firearm-possession permit required to possess gun at home?	Yes[2]	2C:39/58
Firearm-possession permit required to possess gun at work?	No	2C:39/58
Gun owner's identification card or firearm-purchase-approval permit required before a resident may buy a handgun?	Yes	2C:39/58
Are firearms required to be registered with state police or similar firearms-registration bureau?	No[3]	2C:58-3(e)
Waiting period after handgun purchase?	30 days[4]	2C:58-3(f)

1. Issued primarily only to policemen.
2. For Semi-automatic, military-style firearms only.
3. Handgun sales reported to local police. Semi-automatics must be registered with police.
4. Permit good for 90 days. 45-day wait for non-residents.
NOTE: As city or county gun-control codes may be more restrictive than state law, inquire of your local police about how local codes affect your possession and use of firearms.

New Mexico
Constitutional guarantee: No law shall abridge the right of the citizen to keep and bear arms for security and defense, for lawful hunting and recreational use, and for other lawful purposes, but nothing herein shall be held to permit the carrying of concealed weapons. [Art. 2, sec. 6]1

Self-defense code: 30-2-7
Homicide is justifiable when committed by any person in any of the following cases: A. when committed in the necessary defense of his life, his family or his property, or in necessarily defending against any unlawful action directed against himself, his wife, or family; B. when committed in the lawful defense of himself or of another and when there is reasonable ground to believe a design exists to commit a felony or to do some great personal injury against such person or another, and there is imminent danger that the design will be accomplished; or C. when necessarily committed in attempting, by lawful ways and means, to apprehend any person for any felony committed in his presence, or in lawfully suppressing any riot, or in necessarily and lawfully keeping and preserving the peace.

		Code No.
Carrying Concealed Weapons (firearm) permit available?	No[1]	30-7-2
Open holster-gun carrying permissible without license?	Yes	30-7-2
Firearm-possession permit required to possess gun at home?	No	30-7-2
Firearm-possession permit required to possess gun at work?	No	30-7-2
Gun owner's identification card or firearm-purchase-approval permit required before a resident may buy a handgun?	No	
Are firearms required to be registered with state police or similar firearms-registration bureau?	No	
Waiting period after handgun purchase?	None	

1. However, sometimes lawful: see 40A-7-2.
NOTE: As city or county gun-control codes may be more restrictive than state law, inquire of your local police about how local codes affect your possession and use of firearms.

New York

Constitutional guarantee: A well-regulated militia being necessary to the security of a free state, the right of the people to keep and bear arms cannot be infringed. [New York Civil Rights Law, sec. 4]
Self-defense code:

		Code No.
Carrying Concealed Weapons (firearm) permit available?	Yes	265.00
Open holster-gun carrying permissible without license?	No	265.00
Firearm-possession permit required to possess gun at home?	Yes[1]	265.00
Firearm-possession permit required to possess gun at work?	Yes[1]	265.00
Gun owner's identification card or firearm-purchase-approval permit required before a resident may buy a handgun?	Yes[1]	265.00; 400.00.1,.6
Are firearms required to be registered with state police or similar firearms-registration bureau?	Yes[1]	400.00.12
Waiting period after handgun purchase?	Yes[1]	400.00.4-a

1. Handguns only. Up to 6 months for permit to purchase.
NOTE: As city or county gun-control codes may be more restrictive than state law, inquire of your local police about how local codes affect your possession and use of firearms.

North Carolina

Constitutional guarantee: A well-regulated militia being necessary to the security of a free state, the right of the people to keep and bear arms shall not be infringed; and, as standing armies in time of peace are dangerous to liberty, they shall not be maintained, and the military shall be kept under strict subordination to, and governed by, the civil power. Nothing herein shall justify the practice of carrying concealed weapons, or prevent the General Assembly from enacting penal statutes against that practice. [Art. 1, sec. 30]

Self-defense code: *State v. Todd*, 264 NC 524, 142 SE 2d 154 (1965).

Carrying Concealed Weapons (firearm) permit available?	No[1]	14-269
Open holster-gun carrying permissible without license?	No	14-269
Firearm-possession permit required to possess gun at home?	No	14-269
Firearm-possession permit required to possess gun at work?	No	
Gun owner's identification card or firearm-purchase-approval permit required before a resident may buy a handgun?	Yes[2]	14-402
Are firearms required to be registered with state police or similar firearms-registration bureau?	Yes[3]	14-407
Waiting period after handgun purchase?	None[4]	

1. Possession of an unconcealed pistol in an automobile is not a violation of this statute; see atty. gen. opinion to

Sheriff Albert Jackson (Henderson Co.), 41 NCAG 207 (1971).

2. Handguns only.

3. Registered for taxation purposes.

4. Up to thirty-day wait for permit to purchase.

NOTE: As city or county gun-control codes may be more restrictive than state law, inquire of your local police about how local codes affect your possession and use of firearms.

North Dakota

Constitutional guarantee: All individuals are by nature equally free and independent and have certain inalienable rights, among which are ... to keep and bear arms for the defense of their person, family, property, and the state, and for lawful hunting, recreational, and other lawful purposes, which shall not be infringed. [Article I, Section 30.]

Self-defense code: 12.1-0501 thru 09

1. A person is not justified in using more force than is necessary and appropriate under the circumstances. 2. Deadly force is justified in the following instances: ... b. When used in lawful self-defense, or in lawful defense of others, if such force is necessary to protect the actor or anyone else against death, serious bodily injury, or the commission of a felony involving violence. The use of deadly force is not justified if it can be avoided, with safety to the actor and others, by retreat or other conduct involving minimal interference with the freedom of the person menaced. A person seeking to protect someone else must, before using deadly force, try to cause that person to retreat, or otherwise comply with the requirements of this provision, if safety can be obtained thereby. But...(2) no person is required to retreat from his dwelling, or place of work, unless he was the original aggressor or is assailed by a person who he knows also dwells or works there...

		Code No.
Carrying Concealed Weapons (firearm) permit available?	Yes	62-01-07
Open holster-gun carrying permissible without license?	No	62-0105
Firearm-possession permit required to possess gun at home?	No	62-01-05
Firearm-possession permit required to possess gun at work?	No	62-01-05
Gun owner's identification card or firearm-purchase-approval permit required before a resident may buy a handgun?	No	
Are firearms required to be registered with state police or similar firearms-registration bureau?	No[1]	62-01-09
Waiting period after handgun purchase?	None	

1. Handgun sales reported to state Bureau of Criminal Investigation within 7 days of transfer.

NOTE: As city or county gun-control codes may be more restrictive than state law, inquire of your local police about how local codes affect your possession and use of firearms.

Ohio

Constitutional guarantee: The people have the right to bear arms for their defense and security; but standing armies, in time of peace, are dangerous to liberty, and shall not be kept up; and the military shall be in strict subordination to the civil power. [Art. 1, sec. 4]

Self-defense code: ORC 2901.05

See: *State v. Robinson*, 470 2S 103 (1976)

		Code No.
Carrying Concealed Weapons (firearm) permit available?	No[1]	2923.12
Open holster-gun carrying permissible without license?	No	2923.12
Firearm-possession permit required to possess gun at home?	No	2923.12(c)2
Firearm-possession permit required to possess gun at work?	No	2923.12(c)
Gun owner's identification card or firearm-purchase-approval permit required before a resident may buy a handgun?	No	
Are firearms required to be registered with state police or similar firearms-registration bureau?	No	
Waiting period after handgun purchase?	None	

1. Civilians may not carry concealed firearms, and there is no state permit that would allow them to do so.

NOTE: As city or county gun-control codes may be more restrictive than state law, inquire of your local police about how local codes affect your possession and use of firearms.

Oklahoma

Constitutional guarantee: The right of a citizen to keep and bear arms in the defense of his home, person, or property, or in aid of the civil power, when thereunto legally summoned, shall never be prohibited; but nothing herein contained shall prevent the legislature for regulating the carrying of weapons. [Art. 3, sec. 26]

Self-defense code: 21-733

Homicide is also justifiable when committed by any person in either of the following cases: 1. When resisting any attempt to murder such person or to commit any felony upon him, or upon or in any dwelling house in which such person is; or, 2. When committed in the lawful defense of such person, or of his or her husband, wife, parent, child, master, mistress, or servant, when there is reasonable ground to apprehend a design to commit a felony, or to do some great personal injury, and imminent danger of such design being accomplished; or 3. When necessarily committed in attempting, by lawful ways and means, to apprehend any person for any felony committed; or in lawfully suppressing any riot; or in lawfully keeping and preserving the peace.

		Code No.
Carrying Concealed Weapons (firearm) permit available?	No[1]	1271
Open holster-gun carrying permissible without license?	Yes[2]	1271
Firearm-possession permit required to possess gun at home?	No	
Firearm-possession permit required to possess gun at work?	No	
Gun owner's identification card or firearm-purchase-approval permit required before a resident may buy a handgun?	No	
Are firearms required to be registered with state police or similar firearms-registration bureau?	No	
Waiting period after handgun purchase?	None	

1. Civilians may not carry handguns concealed, or in a holster.
2. Unloaded only.
NOTE: As city or county gun-control codes may be more restrictive than state law, inquire of your local police about how local codes affect your possession and use of firearms.

Oregon

Constitutional guarantee: The people shall have the right to bear arms for the defense of themselves, and the state, but the military shall be kept in strict subordination to the civil power. [Art. 1, sec. 27]
Self-defense code:

		Code No.
Carrying Concealed Weapons (firearm) permit available?	Yes	166.290
Open holster-gun carrying permissible without license?	Yes	166.290
Firearm-possession permit required to possess gun at home?	No	
Firearm-possession permit required to possess gun at work?	No	
Gun owner's identification card or firearm-purchase-approval permit required before a resident may buy a handgun?	No	
Are firearms required to be registered with state police or similar firearms-registration bureau?	Yes[1]	16.420
Waiting period after handgun purchase?	15 days[2]	

1. Only handgun sales need to be reported to local police.
2. Zero days with permit to carry concealed weapons.

NOTE: As city or county gun-control codes may be more restrictive than state law, inquire of your local police about how local codes affect your possession and use of firearms.

Pennsylvania

Constitutional guarantee: The right of the citizens to bear arms in defense of themselves and the state shall not be questioned. [Art. 1, sec. 21]

Self-defense code: 18 CPSA sec. 507 Pub. L. 707 No. with amendment 1980-235

		Code No.
Carrying Concealed Weapons (firearm) permit available?	Yes	18 CPSA
Open holster-gun carrying permissible without license?	No	18 CPSA
Firearm-possession permit required to possess gun at home?	No	18 CPSA
Firearm-possession permit required to possess gun at work?	No	18 CPSA
Gun owner's identification card or firearm-purchase-approval permit required before a resident may buy a handgun?	Yes[1]	6111(a)
Are firearms required to be registered with state police or similar firearms-registration bureau?	No	18 CPSA
Waiting period after handgun purchase?	2 days[1]	6111(a)

1. Includes all long arms.

NOTE: As city or county gun-control codes may be more restrictive than state law, inquire of your local police about how local codes affect your possession and use of firearms.

Rhode Island

Constitutional guarantee: The right of the people to keep and bear arms shall not be infringed. [Art. 1, sec. 2]

Self-defense code: 11-8-8

In the event that any person shall die or shall sustain a personal injury in any way or for any cause while in the commission of any criminal offense enumerated in sec. 11-8-2 through 11-8-6 inclusive, it shall be presumed as a matter of law in any civil or criminal proceeding, that the owner, tenant, or occupier of the place wherein the offense was committed, acted in self-defense at the time and place where the death of the person or the injury to the person was inflicted, caused or sustained; provided, however, that said presumption shall be rebuttal.

		Code No.
Carrying Concealed Weapons (firearm) permit available?	Yes	11-47-11
Open holster-gun carrying permissible without license?	No	11-47-8
Firearm-possession permit required to possess gun at home?	No	11-47-8
Firearm-possession permit required to possess gun at work?	No	11-47-8
Gun owner's identification card or firearm-purchase-approval permit required before a resident may buy a handgun?	Yes[1]	11-47-35
Are firearms required to be registered with state police or similar firearms-registration bureau?	No	11-47-41
Waiting period after handgun purchase?	7 days	11-47-35(a)

1. Purchaser must show evidence of completing state safety course.

NOTE: As city or county gun-control codes may be more restrictive than state law, inquire of your local police about how local codes affect your possession and use of firearms.

South Carolina

Constitutional guarantee: A well-regulated militia, being necessary to the security of a free state, the right of the people to keep and bear arms, shall not be infringed. [Art. 1, sec. 20]

Self-defense code: 16-3-40

		Code No.
Carrying Concealed Weapons (firearm) permit available?	Yes	23-31-120
Open holster-gun carrying permissible without license?	No	16-23-20
Firearm-possession permit required to possess gun at home?	No	16-23-20
Firearm-possession permit required to possess gun at work?	No	16-23-20
Gun owner's identification card or firearm-purchase-approval permit required before a resident may buy a handgun?	No[1]	
Are firearms required to be registered with state police or similar firearms-registration bureau?	No[2]	
Waiting period after handgun purchase?	None	23-31-140

1. One pistol purchase per month.
2. Handgun sales reported to state police.

NOTE: As city or county gun-control codes may be more restrictive than state law, inquire of your local police about how local codes affect your possession and use of firearms.

South Dakota

Constitutional guarantee: The right of citizens to bear arms in defense of themselves and the state shall not be denied. [Art. 6, sec. 24]

Self-defense code: 22-16-33 thru 35

(22-16-33) Homicide is justifiable when necessarily committed in attempting by lawful ways and means to apprehend any person for any felony committed, or in lawfully suppressing any riot, or in lawfully keeping and preserving the peace. (22-16-34) Homicide is justifiable when committed by any person when resisting any attempt to murder such person, or to commit any felony upon him or her, or in any dwelling house in which such person is. (22-16-35) Homicide is justifiable when committed by any person in the lawful defense of such person, or of his or her husband, wife, parent, child, master, mistress, or servant when there is reasonable ground to apprehend a design to commit a felony, or to do some great personal injury, and imminent danger of such design being accomplished.

		Code No.
Carrying Concealed Weapons (firearm) permit available?	Yes	23-7-7
Open holster-gun carrying permissible without license?	No	23-14-9
Firearm-possession permit required to possess gun at home?	No	22-14-11
Firearm-possession permit required to possess gun at work?	No	22-14-11
Gun owner's identification card or firearm-purchase-approval permit required	Yes	23-7-10

before a resident may buy
a handgun?

Are firearms required to be   No[1]   23-7-10
registered with state police
or similar firearms-
registration bureau?

Waiting period after   2 days[2] 23-7-9
handgun purchase?

1. Handgun sales reported to local police and secretary of state; records are kept for six years.
2. Zero days with CCW.

NOTE: As city or county gun-control codes may be more restrictive than state law, inquire of your local police about how local codes affect your possession and use of firearms.

Tennessee

Constitutional guarantee: That the citizens of this state have a right to keep and bear arms for their common defense; but the legislature shall have power, by law, to regulate the wearing of arms with a view to prevent crime. [Art. 1, sec. 26]

Self-defense code:

		Code No.
Carrying Concealed Weapons (firearm) permit available?	No[1]	39-4901
Open holster-gun carrying permissible without license?	No	39-4901
Firearm-possession permit required to possess gun at home?	No	
Firearm-possession permit required to possess gun at work?	No	
Gun owner's identification card or firearm-purchase-approval permit required before a resident may buy	Yes	39-6-1704(c)

a handgun?

Are firearms required to be registered with state police or similar firearms-registration bureau?	No[2]	39-4904
Waiting period after handgun purchase?	15 days	39-6-1704(c)

1. Permits exist, but issued only to policemen, firemen, and private security guards, civilians may not carry concealed.
2. Handgun sales only, reported to local police.

NOTE: As city or county gun-control codes may be more restrictive than state law, inquire of your local police about how local codes affect your possession and use of firearms.

Texas

Constitutional guarantee: Every citizen shall have the right to keep and bear arms in the lawful defense of himself or the state, but the legislature shall have power, by law, to regulate the wearing of arms, with a view to prevent crime. [Art. 1, sec. 23]

Self-defense code:

		Code No.
Carrying Concealed Weapons (firearm) permit available?	No[1]	10-46.01
Open holster-gun carrying permissible without license?	No	10-46.01
Firearm-possession permit required to possess gun at home?	No	
Firearm-possession permit required to possess gun at work?	No	
Gun owner's identification card or firearm-purchase-approval permit required before a resident may buy a handgun?	No	

Are firearms required to be registered with state police or similar firearms-registration bureau?	No
Waiting period after handgun purchase?	None

1. Permissible at home or one's business, while traveling or lawfully hunting, see Penal code 46.03.

NOTE: As city or county gun-control codes may be more restrictive than state law, inquire of your local police about how local codes affect your possession and use of firearms.

Utah

Constitutional guarantee: The people have the right to bear arms for their security and defense, but the legislature may regulate the exercise of this right by law. [Art. 1, sec. 6]

Self-defense code: P

		Code No.
Carrying Concealed Weapons (firearm) permit available?	Yes[1]	76-10-513
Open holster-gun carrying permissible without license?	Yes[2]	76-10-505
Firearm-possession permit required to possess gun at home?	No	76-10-510
Firearm-possession permit required to possess gun at work?	No	76-10-510
Gun owner's identification card or firearm-purchase-approval permit required before a resident may buy a handgun?	No	
Are firearms required to be registered with state police or similar firearms-	No	

registration bureau?

Waiting period after handgun purchase?	None

1. Restrictive issuance, few issued.
2. In rural areas only.

NOTE: As city or county gun-control codes may be more restrictive than state law, inquire of your local police about how local codes affect your possession and use of firearms.

Vermont

Constitutional guarantee: That the people have a right to bear arms for the defense of themselves and the state—and as standing armies in time of peace are dangerous to liberty, they ought not to be kept up; and that the military should be kept under strict subordination to and governed by the civil power. [Chap. 1, art. 16]

Self-defense code: T. 13-2305

If a person kills or wounds another under any of the circumstances enumerated below, he shall be guiltless: (1) In the just and necessary defense of his own life or the life of his or her husband, wife, parent, child, brother, sister, master, mistress, servant, guardian, or ward; or (2) In the suppression of a person attempting to commit murder, rape, burglary, or robbery, with force or violences; or (3) In the case of a civil officer; or a military officer or private soldier when lawfully called out to suppress riot or rebellion, or to prevent or suppress invasion, or to assist in serving legal process, in suppressing opposition against him in the just and necessary discharge of his duty.

		Code No.
Carrying Concealed Weapons (firearm) permit available?	Yes[1]	T.13-4003
Open holster-gun carrying permissible without license?	Yes	T.13-4003
Firearm-possession permit required to possess gun at home?	No	

Firearm-possession permit required to possess gun at work?	No	
Gun owner's identification card or firearm-purchase-approval permit required before a resident may buy a handgun?	No	
Are firearms required to be registered with state police or similar firearms-registration bureau?	No[2]	T.13-4006
Waiting period after handgun purchase?	None	

1. No permit exists, but handguns may be carried concealed without the need of a carrying permit.

2. Gunshops must keep records of those who purchase a handgun.

NOTE: As city or county gun-control codes may be more restrictive than state law, inquire of your local police about how local codes affect your possession and use of firearms.

Virginia

Constitutional guarantee: That a well-regulated militia, composed of the body of the people, trained to arms, is the proper, natural, and safe defense of a free state, therefore, the right of the people to keep and bear arms shall not be infringed; that standing armies, in time of peace, should be avoided as dangerous to liberty; and that in all cases the military should be under strict subordination to, and governed by, the civil power. [Art. 1, sec. 13]

Self-defense code: see Michie co. "Code of Virginia," 18.2-32 (B. Defenses) p. 188 (1975)

| | | Code No. |
| Carrying Concealed Weapons (firearm) permit available? | Yes | 18.2-308 |

Open holster-gun carrying permissible without license?	Yes	18.2-308
Firearm-possession permit required to possess gun at home?	No	18.2-308
Firearm-possession permit required to possess gun at work?	No	18.2-308
Gun owner's identification card or firearm-purchase-approval permit required before a resident may buy a handgun?	No	
Are firearms required to be registered with state police or similar firearms-registration bureau?	No	
Waiting period after handgun purchase?	None	

NOTE: As city or county gun-control codes may be more restrictive than state law, inquire of your local police about how local codes affect your possession and use of firearms.

Washington (State)
Constitutional guarantee: The right of the individual citizen to bear arms in defense of himself, or the state, shall not be impaired, but nothing in this section shall be construed as authorizing individuals or corporations to organize, maintain, or employ an armed body of men. [Art 1, sec. 24]
Self-defense code: RCW 9A.16.050
Homicide is also justifiable when committed either: (1) In the lawful defense of the slayer [i.e., victim], or his or her husband, wife, parent, brother, or sister, or any other person in his presence or company, when there is reasonable ground to apprehend a design on the part of the person slain to commit a felony or to do some great

personal injury to the slayer or to any such person, and there is imminent danger of such design being accomplished; or (2) In the actual residence of an attempt to commit a felony upon the slayer, in his presence, or upon or in a dwelling, or other place of abode in which he is.

		Code No.
Carrying Concealed Weapons (firearm) permit available?	Yes	9.41.070
Open holster-gun carrying permissible without license?	Yes[1]	9.41.050
Firearm-possession permit required to possess gun at home?	No	
Firearm-possession permit required to possess gun at work?	No	
Gun owner's identification card or firearm-purchase-approval permit required before a resident may buy a handgun?	No	9.41.090
Are firearms required to be registered with state police or similar firearms-registration bureau?	No[2]	
Waiting period after handgun purchase?	5 days[3]	9.41.090

1. Legal, but not advisable. According to the Seattle Police, you will be arrested under the intimidation law.
2. Handgun sale reported to local police and state Bureau of Firearm Licensing; records kept for seven years.
3. Zero days with CCW permit. 60 days for non-residents.

West Virginia
Constitutional guarantee: a person has the right to keep and bear arms for the defense of self, family, home, and

state, and for lawful hunting and recreational use. [Art. II, Sect. 22]

Self-defense code: see Michie Co. "West Virginia Code," 61-2-1 (v. Self-defense), pp. 014-5 (1977)

		Code No.
Carrying Concealed Weapons (firearm) permit available?	Yes	67-7-2
Open holster-gun carrying permissible without license?	No	67-7-1
Firearm-possession permit required to possess gun at home?	No	67-7-3
Firearm-possession permit required to possess gun at work?	No	67-7-3
Gun owner's identification card or firearm-purchase-approval permit required before a resident may buy a high powered rifle?	Yes	61-7-8
Are firearms required to be registered with state police or similar firearms-registration bureau?	No[1]	67-7-9
Waiting period after handgun purchase?	None	

1. Gunshops must record those who purchase a handgun, report to state police.

NOTE: As city or county gun-control codes may be more restrictive than state law, inquire of your local police about how local codes affect your possession and use of firearms.

Wisconsin
Constitutional guarantee: none
Self-defense code: 939.48-939.49

		Code No.
Carrying Concealed Weapons (firearm) permit available?	No[1]	941-23
Open holster-gun carrying permissible without license?	Yes	941.23
Firearm-possession permit required to possess gun at home?	No	
Firearm-possession permit required to possess gun at work?	No	
Gun owner's identification card or firearm-purchase-approval permit required before a resident may buy a handgun?	No	
Are firearms required to be registered with state police or similar firearms-registration bureau?	No[2]	440.95
Waiting period after handgun purchase?	2 days	

1. Civilians may not carry handguns concealed.
2. Only pawnshops or "secondhand" gun stores need to register handgun sales.
NOTE: As city or county gun-control codes may be more restrictive than state law, inquire of your local police about how local codes affect your possession and use of firearms.

Wyoming
Constitutional guarantee: The right of citizens to bear arms in defense of themselves and their state shall not be denied. [Art. 1, sec. 24]
Self-defense code: 6-11-102

		Code No.
Carrying Concealed Weapons (firearm) permit available?	Yes	6-11-103

Open holster-gun carrying permissible without license?	No	6-11-103
Firearm-possession permit required to possess gun at home?	No	
Firearm-possession permit required to possess gun at work?	No	
Gun owner's identification card or firearm-purchase-approval permit required before a resident may buy a handgun?	No	
Are firearms required to be registered with state police or similar firearms-registration bureau?	No	6-11-107
Waiting period after handgun purchase?	None	

NOTE: As city or county gun-control codes may be more restrictive than state law, inquire of your local police about how local codes affect your possession and use of firearms.

Appendix A

Bibliography of Progun Books and Articles

Ayoob, Massad, *Armed and Alive* (Bellevue, WA.: Second Amendment Foundation), 1980.

_____ . *In the Gravest Extreme: The Role of the Firearm in Personal Protection,* 1979 (Box 122, Concord, NH. 03301).

_____ . *The Truth About Self-Protection* (New York, NY.: Bantam), 1983.

Bruce-Briggs, Barry, "The Great American Gun War," *Public Interest,* Fall 1976, p. 37.

Drooz, Richard, "Handguns and Hokum: A Methodological Problem," *Journal of the American Medical Association,* July 4, 1977, p. 43.

Edwards, James, *Myths About Guns* (Coral Springs, FL.: Peninsula Press), 1978.

FBI, *Uniform Crime Reports for the U.S.* (Washington, D.C.: U.S. Government Printing Office), annual.

Feder, Donald, "A Libertarian Look at Gun Control," *Reason,* March 1979, p. 24.

Gottlieb, Alan, *Gun Rights Fact Book* (Bellevue, WA.: Merril Press), 1988.

_____ . *The Gun Grabbers* (Bellevue, WA.: Merril Press), 1991.

Greenwood, Colin, *Firearms Control* (London: Routledge & Kegan Paul), 1972.

Halbrook, Stephen P., *That Every Man Be Armed: The Evolution of a Constitutional Right* (Albuquerque, NM.: University of New Mexico Press), 1984.

Hardy, David, *The BATF's War on Civil Liberties: The Assault on*

Gun Owners (Bellevue, WA.: Second Amendment Foundation), 1979.

_____ . *No Case for Stricter Handgun Controls* (Bellevue, WA.: Second Amendment Foundation), 1978.

Jepsen, Roger, "DMI (Progun) Poll," *Congressional Record*, March 26, 1979, p. S3398.

Kates, Donald, "Against Civil Disarmament," *Harper's*, September 1978, p. 28.

_____ . "Gun Laws vs. Crime," *Field & Stream*, August 1980, p. 10.

_____ . (ed) *Restricting Handguns: The Liberal Skeptics Speak Out* (Croton-on-Hudson, NY.: North River Press), 1979.

_____ . "Why a Civil Libertarian Opposes Gun Control," *Civil Liberties Review*, June-July 1976, p. 24.

Kessler, Raymond, "Enforcement Problems of Gun Control," *Criminal Law Bulletin*, March-April 1980, p. 133.

Kleck, Gary, *The Good Side of Guns: The Role of Firearms in Self-defense* (Bellevue, WA.: Second Amendment Foundation), 1988.

Krug, Alan, "The Misuse of Firearms in Crime," *Gun Week*, March 28, 1980, p. 4.

Kukla, Robert, *Gun Control* (Harrisburg, PA.: Stackpole Books), 1973.

Leddy, Edward (ed), *Journal of Firearms and Public Policy* (Bellevue, WA.: Second Amendment Foundation), Annual.

Levinson, Stanford, "The Embarrassing Second Amendment," *99 Yale Law Journal 3*, December, 1989, p. 637.

Lewis, John, " American Gestapo," *Reason*, April 1980, p. 24.

Mahoney, R.J., "The Morality of Home Defense," *Guns for Home Defense* (Los Angeles, CA.: Peterson Publishing), 1975.

Nisbet, Lee, (ed) *The Gun Control Debate: You Decide* (Buffalo, NY.: Prometheus), 1990.

Reynolds, Morgan O., *Crime by Choice* (Dallas, TX.: Fisher Institute), 1985.

Tonso, William, (ed) *The Gun Culture and Its Enemies* (Bellevue, WA.: Second Amendment Foundation), 1990.

_____ . *Gun Control: White Man's Law* (Bellevue, WA.: Second Amendment Foundation), 1985.

Whisker, James, "Historical Evolution and Subsequent Erosion

of the Right to Keep and Bear Arms," *78 West Virginia Law Review*
1, December 1975, p. 171.

_____ . *Our Vanishing Freedom* (McLean, VA.: Heritage House
Publishers), 1972.

_____ . *The Right to Hunt* (Croton-on-Hudson, NY.: North
River Press), 1981.

Appendix B

Progun Journals

American Firearms Industry
7001 N. Clark St.
Chicago, IL 60626

American Handgunner
591 Camino de la Reina,
Suite 200
San Diego, CA 92108

American Hunter
1600 Rhode Island Ave.
Washington, DC 20036

American Rifleman
470 Spring Park Place #1000
Herndon, VA 22070

Field & Stream
2 Park Avenue
New York, NY 10016

Gun Week
267 Linwood Avenue
Buffalo, NY 14209

Gun World
34240 Camino Capistrano
Capistrano Beach, CA 92624

Guns
591 Camino de la Reina
San Diego, CA 92108

Guns & Ammo
8490 Sunset Blvd. #204
Los Angeles, CA 90069

Handloader
6471 Airpark Drive
Prescott, AZ 86301

Journal of Firearms and Public Policy
12500 N.E. Tenth Place
Bellevue, WA 98005

Outdoor Life
2 Park Avenue
New York, NY 10016

Petersen's Hunting
8490 Sunset Blvd.
Los Angeles, CA 90069

Precision Shooting
37 Burnham Street
East Hartford, CT 06108

Point Blank
(Citizens Committee for the
Right to Keep & Bear Arms)
Liberty Park
12500 N.E. Tenth Place
Bellevue, WA 98004

Political Gun News
7777 Leesburg Pike
Falls Church, VA 22043

Rifle
6471 Airpark Drive
Prescott, AZ 89301

Second Amendment Reporter
(Second Amendment Foun-
dation)
12500 N.E. Tenth Place
Bellevue, WA 98005

Shooting Industry
591 Camino de la Reina
San Diego, CA 92108

Shooting Times
News Plaza
Box 1790
Peoria, IL 61656

Shotgun Sports
11770 Jones Street #102
Auburn CA 95603

Women & Guns
12500 N.E. Tenth Place
Bellevue, WA 98005

Appendix C

State-by-State BATF Field Offices

For Assistance with Applications, Records, Transactions, and Other Regulatory Matters, Address Your Questions to the "Area Supervisor," "Bureau of Alcohol, Tobacco, and Firearms," at the Office in Your State.

ALABAMA
Birmingham: 600 Beacon Ridge Parkway West, Suite 730, 35209. 205-731-0040.

ARKANSAS
Little Rock: 700 West Capitol, Rm. 3414, 72201. 501-378-6457.

CALIFORNIA
Fresno: 1130 O St., Rm. 4217, 93721. 209-487-5093.
Los Angeles: Main Post Office, P.O Box 1991, 90053. 213-894-4817.
Sacramento: 801 I St., Room 143, 95814. 916-551-1323.
San Francisco: 651 Brannan St., Room 213, 94107. 415-974-7778.
San Jose: 280 First St., Room 2180, 95113. 408-291-7464.
Santa Ana: P.O. Box 12250, 92712. 714-836-2946.
Santa Rosa: 777 Sonoma Ave., Room 214, 95404. 707-576-0184.

COLORADO
Denver: P.O. Box 3523, Federal Office Building, 80294. 303-844-5027.

CONNECTICUT
Hartford: A.A. Riblcoff Federal Building, 450 Main St., Room 401, 06103. 203-722-2037.

FLORIDA
Miami: 5205 Northwest 84th Ave., Suite 104, 33166. 305-592-9967.

Tampa: 500 Zack St., Room 215, 33602. 813-228-2346.

GEORGIA
Atlanta: 3835 Presidential Parkway, 30340. 404-986-6075.

ILLINOIS
Chicago: 230 S. Dearborn St., 15th Floor, 60604. 312-353-3797.

KENTUCKY
Frankfort: 330 West Broadway, Room 124, 40601. 502-223-3350.

MAINE
Lewiston: 2d Floor, 40 Pine St., 04240 207-786-2577 & 2777

MARYLAND
Baltimore: 31 Hopkins Plaza, Room 938, 21201. 301-962-3200.

MASSACHUSETTS
Boston: Boston Federal Office Building, 10 Causeway St., Room 795, 02222-1079. 617-565-7073.

MICHIGAN

Farmington Hills: Arboretum Building Suite 195, 34505 West Twelve Mile Road, 48331. 313-226-4735.

MINNESOTA

St. Paul: Federal Building and U.S. Courthouse, 316 North Robert St., Room 650, 55101. 612-290-3496.

MISSOURI

Kansas City: 911 Walnut St., Room 1407, 64106. 816-426-2464.

St. Louis: 815 Olive St., Room 310, 63101. 314-539-2251.

NEW JERSEY

Parsippany: 120 Littleton Road, Room 305, 07054. 201-334-7058.

NEW YORK

Buffalo: Federal Building, 111 West Huron St., Room 219, 14202. 716-846-4048.

New York: P.O. Box 3539, Church St. Station, 10008. 212-264-4650.

NORTH CAROLINA

Charlotte: 4630 Park Rd., Suite 441, 28209 704-371-6127.

OHIO

Cincinnati: Holiday Office Park, St. Paul Building Suite 301, 801 B. West 8th St., 45203. 513-684-3351.

Middleburg Heights: Plaza South 1, Room 300, 7251 Engle Road, 44130. 216-522-3374.

OREGON

Portland: 7820 N.E. Holman Suite B-3, 97218. 503-231-2331.

PENNSYLVANIA
Lansdale: Century Plz., 100 West Main St., Suite 300-B, 19446. 215-248-5252.

Pittsburgh: Federal Building, 1000 Liberty Ave., Room 2126, 15222. 412-644-2918.

PUERTO RICO
Hato Rey: Federico Degetau Federal Building, Room 659, Avenida Carlos Chardon, 00918. 809-753-4082.

TEXAS
Dallas: 1100 Commerce St., Room 13C22, 75242. 214-767-9461.

Houston: 333 West Loop North, Suite 111, 77024. 713-220-2157.

San Antonio: 727 E. Durango St., Room A-427, 78206. 512-229-6168.

VIRGINIA
Richmond: P.O. Box 10185, 23240. 804-771-2877.

WASHINGTON
Seattle: Federal Building, 915 Second Ave., Room 842, 98174. 206-442-5900.

WISCONSIN
Milwaukee: 517 East Wisconsin Ave., Room 636, 53202. 414-291-3991.

Appenidix D

1968 Gun Control Act, Title I

(*as Amended by the Firearm Owners' Protection Act of 1986 and other amendments*)

TITLE 1-STATE
FIREARMS CONTROL ASSISTANCE

PURPOSE

SEC. 101. The Congress hereby declares that the purpose of this title is to provide support to Federal, State, and local law enforcement officials in their fight against crime and violence, and it is not the purpose of this title to place any undue or unnecessary Federal restrictions or burdens on law-abiding citizens with respect to the acquisition, possession, or use of firearms appropriate to the purpose of hunting, trapshooting, target shooting, personal protection, or any other lawful activity, and that this title is not intended to discourage or eliminate the private ownership or use of firearms by law-abiding citizens for lawful purposes, or provide for the imposition by Federal regulations of any procedures or requirements other than those reasonably necessary to implement and effectuate the provisions of this title.

Public Law 99-308
An Act to amend chapter 44 (relating to firearms) of title 18, United States Code, and for other purposes.
Be it enacted by the Senate and House of Representatives

of the United States of America in Congress assembled,

SECTION 1. SHORT TITLE AND CONGRESSIONAL FINDINGS.

(a) SHORT TITLE.- This act may be cited as the "Firearms Owners' Protection Act".

CHAPTER 44-FIREARMS

921. Definitions

(a) As used in this chapter-

(1) The term **"person"** and the term **"whoever"** include any individual, corporation, company, association, firm, partnership, society, or joint stock company.

(2) The term **"interstate or foreign commerce"** includes commerce between any place in a State and any place outside of the State, or within any possession of the United States (not including the Canal Zone) or the District of Columbia, but such term does not include commerce between places within the same State but through any place outside of that State. The term **"State"** includes the District of Columbia, the Commonwealth of Puerto Rico, and the possessions of the United States (not including the Canal Zone).

(3) The term **"firearm"** means

(A) any weapon (including a starter gun) which will or is designed to or may readily be converted to expel a projectile by the action of an explosive;

(B) the frame or receiver of any such weapon;

(C) any firearm muffler or firearm silencer; or

(D) any destructive device. Such term does not include an antique firearm.

(4) the term **"destructive device"** means-

(A) any explosive, incendiary, or poison gas-

(i) bomb,

(ii) grenade,

(iii) rocket having a propellant charge of more than four ounces,

(iv) missile having an explosive or incendiary charge of more than one quarter ounce,

(v) mine, or

(vi) device similar to any of the devices described in the preceding clauses;

(B) any type of weapon (other than a shotgun or a shotgun shell which the Secretary finds is generally recognized as particularly suitable for sporting purposes) by whatever name known which will, or which may be readily converted to, expel a projectile by the action of an explosive or other propellant, and which has any barrel with a bore of more than one-half inch in diameter; and

(C) any combination of parts either designed or intended for use in converting any device into any destructive device described in subparagraph (A) or (B) and from which a destructive device may be readily assembled.

The term **"destructive device"** shall not include any device which is neither designed nor redesigned for use as a weapon; any device, although originally designed for use as a weapon, which is redesigned for use as a signaling, pyrotechnic, line throwing, safety, or similar device; surplus ordnance sold, loaned, or given by the Secretary of the Army pursuant to the provisions of section 4684(2), 4685, or 4686 of title 10; or any other device which the Secretary of the Treasury finds is not likely to be used as a weapon, is an antique, or is a rifle which the owner intends to use solely for sporting, recreational or cultural purposes.

(5) The term "shotgun" means a weapon designed or redesigned, made or remade, and intended to be fired from the shoulder and designed or redesigned and made or remade to use the energy of the explosive in a fixed shotgun shell to fire through a smooth bore either a number of ball shot or a single projectile for each single pull of the trigger.

(6) The term "short-barreled shotgun" means a shotgun having one or more barrels less than eighteen inches in length and any weapon made from a shotgun (whether by alteration, modification, or otherwise) if such weapon as modified has an overall length of less than twenty-six inches.

(7) The term "rifle" means a weapon designed or redesigned, made or remade, and intended to be fired from the shoulder and designed or redesigned and made or remade to use the energy of the explosive in a fixed metallic cartridge to fire only a single projectile through a rifled bore for each single pull of the trigger.

(8) The term "short-barreled rifle" means a rifle having one or more barrels less than sixteen inches in length and any weapon made from a rifle (whether by alteration, modification, or otherwise) if such weapon, as modified, has an overall length of less than twenty-six inches.

(9) The term "importer" means any person engaged in the business of importing or bringing firearms or ammunition into the United States for purposes of sale or distribution; and the term "licensed importer" means any

such person licensed under the provisions of this chapter.

(10) The term **"manufacturer"** means any person engaged in the business of manufacturing firearms or ammunition for purposes of sale or distribution; and the term **"licensed manufacturer"** means any such person licensed under the provisions of this chapter.

(11) The term **"dealer"** means

(A) any person engaged in the business of selling firearms at wholesale or retail,

(B) any person engaged in the business of repairing firearms or of making or fitting special barrels, stocks, or trigger mechanisms to firearms, or

(C) any person who is a pawnbroker.

The term **"licensed dealer"** means any dealer who is licensed under the provisions of this chapter.

(12) The term **"pawnbroker"** means any person whose business or occupation includes the taking or receiving, by way of pledge or pawn, of any firearm as security for the payment or repayment of money.

(13) The term **"collector"** means any person who acquires, holds or disposes of firearms as curios or relics, as the Secretary shall by regulation define, and the term **"licensed collector"** means any such person licensed under the provisions of this chapter.

(14) The term **"indictment"** includes an indictment or information in any court under which a crime punishable by imprisonment for a term exceeding one year may be prosecuted.

(15) The term **"fugitive from justice"** means any person who has fled from any State to avoid prosecution for a crime or to avoid giving testimony in any criminal proceeding.

(16) The term **"antique firearm"** means-

(A) any firearm (including any firearm with a matchlock, flintlock, percussion cap, or similar type of ignition system) manufactured in or before 1898; and

(B) any replica of any firearm described in subparagraph (A) if such replica-

(i) is not designed or redesigned for using rimfire or conventional centerfire fixed ammunition, or

(ii) uses rimfire or conventional centerfire fixed ammunition which is no longer manufactured in the United States and which is not readily available in the ordinary channels of commercial trade.

(17)(A) The term "ammunition" means ammunition or cartridge cases, primers, bullets, or propellent powder designed for use in any firearm.

(B) The term "armor piercing ammunition" means a projectile or projectile core which may be used in a handgun and which is constructed entirely (excluding the presence of traces of other substances) from one or a combination of tungsten alloys, steel, iron, brass, bronze, beryllium copper, or depleted uranium. Such term does not include shotgun shot required by Federal or State environmental or game regulations for hunting purposes, a frangible projectile designed for target shooting, a projectile which the Secretary finds is primarily intended to be used for sporting purposes, or any other projectile or projectile core which the Secretary finds is intended to be used for industrial purposes, including a charge used in an oil and gas well perforating device.

(18) The term "Secretary" or "Secretary of the Treasury" means the Secretary of the Treasury or his delegate.

(19) The term "published ordinance" means a published law of any political subdivision of a State which the Secretary determines to be relevant to the enforcement

of this chapter and which is contained on a list compiled by the Secretary, which list shall be published in the Federal Register, revised annually, and furnished to each licensee under this chapter.

(20) The term **"crime punishable by imprisonment for a term exceeding on year"** does not include-

(A) any Federal or State offenses pertaining to antitrust violations, unfair trade practices, restraints of trade, or other similar offenses relating to the regulation of business practices, or

(B) any State offense classified by the laws of the State as a misdemeanor and punishable by a term of imprisonment of two years or less.

What constitutes a conviction of such a crime shall be determined in accordance with the law of the jurisdiction in which the proceedings were held. Any conviction which has been expunged, or set aside or for which a person has been pardoned or has had civil rights restored shall not be considered a conviction for purposes of this chapter, unless such pardon, expungement, or restoration of civil rights expressly provides that the person may not ship, transport, possess, or receive firearms.

(21) The term **"engaged in the business"** means-

(A) As applied to a manufacturer of firearms, a person who devotes time, attention, and labor to manufacturing firearms as a regular course of trade or business with the principal objective of livelihood and profit through the sale or distribution of the firearms manufactured;

(B) as applied to a manufacturer of ammunition, a person who devotes time, attention, and labor to manufacturing ammunition as a regular course of trade or business with the principal objective of livelihood and profit through the sale or distribution of the ammunition manufactured;

(C) as applied to a dealer in firearms, as defined in section 921(a)(11)(A), a person who devotes time, attention, and labor to dealing in firearms as a regular course of trade or business with the principal objective of livelihood and profit through the repetitive purchase and resale of firearms, but such term shall not include a person who makes occasional sales, exchanges, or purchases of firearms for the enhancement of a personal collection or for a hobby, or who sells all or part of his personal collection of firearms;

(D) as applied to a dealer in firearms, as defined in section 921(a)(11)(B), a person who devotes time, attention, and labor to engaging in such activity as regular course of trade or business with the principal objective of livelihood and profit, but such term shall not include a person who makes occasional repairs of firearms, or who occasionally fits special barrels, stocks, or trigger mechanisms to firearms;

(E) as applied to an importer of firearms, a person who devotes time, attention, and labor to importing firearms as a regular course of trade or business with the principal objective of livelihood and profit through the sale or distribution of firearms imported; and

(F) as applied to an importer of ammunition, a person who devotes time, attention, and labor to importing ammunition as a regular course of trade or business with the principal objective of livelihood and profit through the sale or distribution of ammunition imported.

(22) The term "with the principal objective of livelihood and profit" means that the intent underlying the sale or disposition of firearms is predominantly one of obtaining livelihood and pecuniary gain, as opposed to other intents, such as improving or liquidating a personal

firearms collection:

Provided, That proof of profit shall not be required as to a person who engages in the regular and repetitive purchase and disposition of firearms for criminal purposes or terrorism.

For purposes of this paragraph, the term "**terrorism**" means activity, directed against United States persons, which-

(**A**) is committed by an individual who is not a national or permanent resident alien of the United States;

(**B**) involves violent acts or acts dangerous to human life which would be a criminal violation if committed within the jurisdiction of the United States; and

(**C**) is intended-

(**i**) to intimidate or coerce a civilian population;

(**ii**) to influence the policy of a government by intimidation or coercion; or

(**iii**) to affect the conduct of a government by assassination or kidnapping.

(**23**) The term "**machinegun**" has the meaning given such term in section 5845(b) of the National Firearms Act (26 U.S.C. 5845(b)).

(**24**) The terms "**firearm silencer**" and "**firearm muffler**" means any device for silencing, muffling, or diminishing the report of a portable firearm, including any combination of parts, designed or redesigned, and intended for use in assembling or fabricating a firearm silencer or firearm muffler, and any part intended only for use in such assembly or fabrication.

(**b**) For the purposes of this chapter, a member of the Armed Forces on active duty is a resident of the State in which his permanent duty station is located.

(Added Pub.L. 90-351, Title IV SsS 902, June 19, 1968, 82 Stat. 226, and amended Pub.L. 90-618, Title 1, SsS 102, Oct. 22, 1968, 82 Stat. 1214; Pub.L.93-639, SsS 102, Jan. 4, 1975, 88 Stat. 2217; Pub.L. 99-308, Sss 101,

May 19, 1986, 100 Stat. 449; Pub.L. 99-360, SsS 1(b), July 8, 1986, 100 Stat. 766; Pub.L. 99-408, SsS 1, Aug. 28, 1986, 100 Stat. 920.)

922. Unlawful acts.

(a) it shall be unlawful-

(1) for any person-

(A) except a licensed importer, licensed manufacturer, or licensed dealer, to engage in the business of importing, manufacturing, or dealing in firearms, or in the course of such business to ship, transport, or receive any firearm in interstate or foreign commerce; or

(B) except a licensed importer or licensed manufacturer, to engage in the business of importing or manufacturing ammunition, or in the course of such business, to ship, transport, or receive any ammunition in interstate or foreign commerce;

(2) for any importer, manufacturer, dealer, or collector licensed under the provisions of this chapter to ship or transport in interstate or foreign commerce any firearm to any person other than a licensed importer, licensed manufacturer, licensed dealer, or licensed collector, except that-

(A) this paragraph and subsection (b)(3) shall not be held to preclude a licensed importer, licensed manufacturer, licensed dealer, or licensed collector from returning a firearm or replacement firearm of the same kind and type to a person from who it was received; and this paragraph shall not be held to preclude an individual from mailing a firearm owned in compliance with Federal, State, and local law to a licensed importer, licensed dealer, or licensed collector;

(B) this paragraph shall not be held to preclude a licensed importer, licensed manufacturer, or licensed dealer, from depositing a firearm for conveyance in the mails to any officer, employee, agent, or watchman who, pursuant to the provisions of section 1715 of this title, is eligible to receive through the mails pistols, revolvers, and other firearms capable of being concealed on the person, for use in connection with his official duty; and

(C) nothing in this paragraph shall be construed as applying in any manner in the District of Columbia, the Commonwealth of Puerto Rico, or any possession of the United States differently than it would apply if the District of Columbia, the Commonwealth of Puerto Rico, or the possession were in fact a State of the United States;

(3) for any person, other than a licensed importer, licensed manufacturer, licensed dealer, or licensed collector to transport into or receive in the State where he resides (or if the person is a corporation or other business entity, the State where it maintains a place of business) any firearm purchased or otherwise obtained by such person outside that State, except that this paragraph

(A) shall not preclude any person who lawfully acquires a firearm by bequest or interstate succession in a State other than his State of residence from transporting the firearm into or receiving it in the State, if it is lawful for such person to purchase or possess such firearm in that State,

(B) shall not apply to the transportation or receipt of a firearm obtained in conformity with subsection (b)(3) of this section, and

(C) shall not apply to the transportation of any firearm acquired in any State prior to the effective date of this chapter;

(4) for any person, other than a licensed importer, licensed manufacturer, licensed dealer, or licensed collector, to transport in interstate or foreign commerce any destructive device, machinegun (as defined in section 5845 of the Internal Revenue Code of 1954), short-barreled

shotgun, or short-barreled rifle, except as specifically authorized by the Secretary consistent with public safety and necessity;

(5) for any person (other than a licensed importer, licensed manufacturer, licensed dealer, or licensed collector) to transfer, sell, trade, give, transport, or deliver any firearm to any person (other than a licensed importer, licensed manufacturer, licensed dealer, or licensed collector) who the transferor knows or has reasonable cause to believe resides in any State other than that in which the transferor resides (or other than that in which its place of business is located if the transferor is a corporation or other business entity); except that this paragraph shall not apply to

(A) the transfer, transportation, or delivery of a firearm made to carry out a bequest of a firearm to, or an acquisition by interstate succession of a firearm by, a person who is permitted to acquire or possess a firearm under the laws of the State of his residence, and

(B) the loan or rental of a firearm to any person for temporary use for lawful sporting purposes;

(6) for any person in connection with the acquisition or attempted acquisition of any firearm or ammunition from a licensed importer, licensed manufacturer, licensed dealer, or licensed collector, knowingly to make any false to fictitious oral or written statement or to furnish or exhibit any false, fictitious or misrepresented identification, intended or likely to deceive such importer, manufacturer, dealer, or collector with respect to any fact material to the lawfulness of the sale or other disposition of such firearm or ammunition under their provisions of this chapter;

(7) for any person to manufacture or import armor piercing ammunition, except that this paragraph shall not apply to-

(A) the manufacture or importation of such ammunition for the use of the United States or any department or agency thereof or any State or any department, agency, or political subdivision thereof;

(B) the manufacture of such ammunition for the purpose of exportation; and

(C) any manufacture or importation for the purposes of testing or experimentation authorized by the Secretary; and

(8) for any manufacturer or importer to sell or deliver armor piercing ammunition, except that this paragraph shall not apply to-

(A) the sale or delivery by a manufacturer or importer of such ammunition for use of the United States or any department or agency thereof or any State or any department, agency, or political subdivision thereof;

(B) the sale or delivery by a manufacturer or importer of such ammunition for the purpose exportation.

(C) the sale or delivery by a manufacturer or importer of such ammunition for the purposes of testing or experimenting authorized by the Secretary.

(b) it shall be unlawful for any licensed importer, licensed manufacturer, licensed dealer, or licensed collector to sell or deliver-

(1) any firearm or ammunition to any individual who the licensee knows or has reasonable cause to believe is less than eighteen years of age, and, if the firearm, or ammunition is other than a shotgun or rifle, or ammunition for a shotgun or rifle, to any individual who the licensee knows or has reasonable cause to believe is less than twenty-one years of age;

(2) any firearm to any person in any State where the purchase or possession by such person of such firearm

would be in violation of any State law or any published ordinance applicable at the place of sale, delivery or other disposition, unless the licensee knows or has reasonable cause to believe that the purchase or possession would not be in violation of such State law or such published ordinance;

(3) any firearm to any person who the licensee knows or has reasonable cause to believe does not reside in (or if the person is a corporation or other business entity, does not maintain a place of business in) the State in which the licensee's place of business is located, except that this paragraph

(A) shall not apply to the sale or delivery of any rifle or shotgun to a resident of a State other than a State in which the licensee's place of business is located if the transferee meets in person with the transferor to accomplish the transfer, and the sale, delivery, and receipt fully comply with the legal conditions of sale in both such States (and any licensed manufacturer, importer or dealer shall be presumed, for purposes of this subparagraph, in the absence of evidence to the contrary, to have had actual knowledge of the State laws and published ordinances of both States), and

(B) shall not apply to the loan or rental of a firearm to any person for temporary use for lawful sporting purposes;

(4) to any person any destructive device, machinegun (as defined in section 5845 of the Internal Revenue Code of 1954), short-barreled shotgun, or short-barreled rifle, except as specifically authorized by the Secretary consistent with public safety and necessity; and

(5) any firearm or armor-piercing ammunition to any person unless the licensee notes in his record, required to be kept pursuant to section 923 of this chapter, the name, age and place of residence of such person if the person is

an individual, or the identity and principal and local places of business of such person if the person is a corporation or other business entity.

Paragraphs (1), (2), (3), and (4) of this subsection shall not apply to transactions between licensed importers, licensed manufacturers, licensed dealers, and licensed collectors. Paragraph (4) of this subsection shall not apply to a sale or delivery to any research organization designated by the Secretary.

(c) In any case not otherwise prohibited by this chapter, a licensed importer, licensed manufacturer, or licensed dealer may sell a firearm to a person who does not appear in person at the licensees business premises (other than another licensed importer, manufacture, or dealer) only if-

(1) the transferee submits to the transferor a sworn statement in the following form:

"Subject to penalties provided by law, I swear that, in the case of any firearm other than a shotgun or a rifle, I am twenty-one years of more of age, or that, in the case of a shotgun or a rifle, I am eighteen years or more of age: that I am not prohibited by the provisions of chapter 44 of title 18, United States Code, from receiving a firearm in interstate or foreign commerce; and that my receipt of this firearm will not be in violation of any statute of the State and published ordinance applicable to the locality in which I reside. Further, the true title, name, and address of the principal law enforcement officer of the locality to which the firearm will be delivered are_____

Signature_____,

Date_____."

and containing blank space for the attachment of a true copy of any permit or other information required pursuant to such statue or published ordinance:

(2) the transferor has, prior to the shipment or delivery of the firearm, forwarded by registered or certified mail (return receipt requested) a copy of the sworn statement, together with a description of the firearm, in a form prescribed by the Secretary, to the chief law enforcement officer of the transferee's place of residence, and has received a return receipt evidencing delivery of the statement or has had the statement returned due to the refusal of the named addressee to accept such letter in accordance with United States Post Office Department regulations; and

(3) the transferor has delayed shipment or delivery for a period of at least seven days following receipt of the notification of the acceptance or refusal of delivery of the statement.

A copy of the sworn statement and a copy of the notification to the local law enforcement office, together with evidence of receipt or rejection of that notification shall be retained by the licensee as a part of the records required to be kept under section 923(g).

(d) It shall be unlawful for any person to sell or otherwise dispose of any firearm or ammunition to any person knowing or having reasonable cause to believe that such person-

(1) is under indictment for, or has been convicted in any court of, a crime punishable by imprisonment for a term exceeding one year;

(2) is a fugitive from justice;

(3) is an unlawful user of or addicted to any controlled substance (as defined in section 102 of the Controlled Substance Acts (21 U.S.C. 802));

(4) has been adjudicated as a mental defective or has been committed to any mental institution;

(5) who, being an alien, is illegally or unlawfully in the United State;

(6) who has been discharged from the Armed

Forces under dishonorable conditions; or

(7) who, having been a citizen of the United States, has renounced his citizenship.

This subsection shall not apply with respect to the sale or disposition of a firearm or ammunition to a licensed importer, licensed manufacturer, licensed dealer, or licensed collector who pursuant to subsection (b) of section 925 of this chapter is not precluded from dealing in firearms or ammunition, or to a person who has been granted relief from disabilities pursuant to subsection (c) of section 925 of this chapter.

(e) It shall be unlawful for any person knowingly to deliver or cause to be delivered to any common or contract carrier for transportation or shipment in interstate or foreign commerce, to persons other than licensed importers, licensed manufacturers, licensed dealers, or licensed collectors, any package or other container in which there is any firearm or ammunition without written notice to the carrier that such firearm or ammunition is being transported or shipped; except that any passenger who owns or legally possesses a firearm or ammunition being transported aboard any common or contract carrier for movement with the passenger in interstate or foreign commerce may deliver said firearm or ammunition into the custody of the pilot, captain, conductor or operator of such common or contract carrier for the duration of the trip without violating any of the provisions of this chapter.

(f) it shall be unlawful for any common or contract carrier to transport or deliver in interstate or foreign commerce any firearm or ammunition with knowledge or reasonable cause to believe that the shipment, transportation, or receipt thereof would be in violation of the provisions of this chapter.

(g) It shall be unlawful for any person-

(1) who has been convicted in any court of a crime punishable by imprisonment for a term exceeding one

year;

(2) Who is a fugitive from justice;

(3) [who] is an unlawful user of or addicted to any controlled substance (as defined in section 102 of the Controlled Substances Act (21 U.S.c. 802));

(4) who has been adjudicated as a mental defective or who has been committed to a mental institution;

(5) who, being an alien, is illegally or unlawfully in the United States;

(6) who has been discharged from the Armed Forces under dishonorable conditions; or

(7) who, having been a citizen of the United States, has renounced his citizenship;

to ship or transport in interstate or foreign commerce, or possess in or affecting commerce, any firearm or ammunition; or to receive any firearm or ammunition which has been shipped or transported in interstate or foreign commerce.

(h) It shall be unlawful for any individual, who to that individual's knowledge and while being employed for any person described in any paragraph of subsection (g) of this section, in the course of such employment-

(1) to receive, possess, or transport any firearm or ammunition in or affecting interstate or foreign commerce; or

(2) to receive any firearm or ammunition which has been shipped or transported in interstate or foreign commerce.

(i) It shall be unlawful for any person to transport or ship in interstate or foreign commerce, any stolen firearm or stolen ammunition, knowing or having reasonable cause to believe that the firearm or ammunition was stolen.

(j) It shall be unlawful for any person to receive, conceal, store, barter, sell, or dispose of any stolen firearm or stolen ammunition, or pledge or accept as security for a loan any stolen firearm or stolen ammunition, which is moving as, which is a part of, or which constitutes, interstate or foreign commerce, knowing or having reasonable cause to believe that the firearm or ammunition was stolen.

(k) It shall be unlawful for any person knowingly to transport, ship, or receive, in interstate or foreign commerce, any firearm which has had the importer's or manufacturer's serial number removed, obliterated, or altered.

(l) Except as provided in section 925(d) of this chapter, it shall be unlawful for any person knowingly to import or bring into the United States or any possession thereof any firearm or ammunition; and it shall be unlawful for any person knowingly to receive any firearm or ammunition which has been imported or brought into the United States or any possession thereof in violation of the provisions of this chapter.

(m) It shall be unlawful for any licensed importer, licensed manufacturer, licensed dealer, or licensed collector knowingly to make any false entry in, to fail to make appropriate entry in, or to fail to properly maintain, any record which he is required to keep pursuant to section 923 of this chapter or regulations promulgated thereunder.

(n) It shall be unlawful for any person who is under indictment for a crime punishable by imprisonment for a term exceeding one year to ship or transport in interstate or foreign commerce any firearm or ammunition or receive any firearm or ammunition which has been shipped or transported in interstate or foreign commerce.

(o)(1) Except as provided in paragraph (2), it shall be unlawful for any person to transfer or possess a machinegun.

(2) This subsection does not apply with respect to-

(A) a transfer to or by, or possession by or under the authority of, the United States or any department or agency thereof or a State, or a department, agency, or political subdivision thereof; or

(B) any lawful transfer or lawful possession of a machinegun that was lawfully possessed before the date this subsection takes effect.

(Added Pub.L. 90-351, Title IV 902, June 19, 1968, 82 Stat. 228, and amended Pub.L. 90-618, Title 1, 102, Oct. 22, 1968, 82 Stat. 1216; Pub.L. 97-377, Title 1, 165(a), Dec. 21, 1982, 96 Stat. 1923; Pub.L. 99-308, 102 May 19, 1986, 100 Stat. 451; Pub.L. 99-408, Aug. 28, 1986, 100 Stat. 920.)

923 Licensing

(a) No person shall engage in the business of importing, manufacturing, or dealing in firearms, or importing or manufacturing ammunition, until he has filed an application with and received a license to do so from the Secretary. The application shall be in such form and contain only that information necessary to determine eligibility for licensing as the Secretary shall by regulation prescribe. Each applicant shall pay a fee for obtaining such a license, a separate fee being required for each place in which the applicant is to do business, as follows:

(1) If the applicant is a manufacturer-

(A) of destructive devices, ammunition for destructive devices or armor piercing ammunition, a fee of $1,000 per year;

(B) of firearms other than destructive devices, a fee of $50 per year; or

(C) of ammunition for firearms, other than ammunition for destructive devices or armor piercing ammunition, a fee of $10 per year.

(2) If the applicant is an importer-

(A) of destructive devices, ammunition for destructive devices or armor piercing ammunition, a fee of $1,000 per year, or

(B) of firearms other than destructive devices or ammunition for firearms other than destructive devices, or ammunition other than armor piercing ammunition, a fee of $50 per year.

(3) If the applicant is a dealer-

(A) in destructive devices or ammunition for destructive devices, a fee of $1,000 per year;

(B) who is a pawnbroker dealing in firearms other than destructive devices a fee of $25 per year; or

(C) who is not a dealer in destructive devices or a pawnbroker, a fee of $10 per year.

(b) Any person desiring to be licensed as a collector shall file an application for such license with the Secretary. The application shall be in such form and contain only that information necessary to determine eligibility as the Secretary shall by regulation prescribe. The fee for such license shall be $10 per year. Any license granted under this subsection shall only apply to transactions in curios and relics.

(c) Upon the filing of a proper application and payment of prescribed fee, the Secretary shall issue to a qualified applicant the appropriate license which, subject to the provisions of this chapter and other applicable provisions of law, shall entitle the licensee to transport, ship, and receive firearms and ammunition covered by such license in interstate or foreign commerce during the period stated in the license. Nothing in this chapter shall be construed to prohibit a licensed manufacturer, importer, or dealer from maintaining and disposing of a personal collection of firearms, subject only to such restrictions as apply in this chapter to dispositions by a person other than a licensed manufacturer, importer, or dealer. If any firearm is so disposed of by a licensee within one year after its transfer from his business inventory into such licensee's personal collection or if such disposition or any other acquisition is made for the purpose of willfully evading the restrictions placed upon licensees by this chapter, then such firearm shall be deemed part of such licensee's business inventory, except that any licensed manufacturer, importer, or dealer who has maintained a firearm as part of a personal collection for one year and who sells or otherwise disposes of such firearm shall record the description of the firearm in a bound volume, containing the name and place of residence and date of birth of the transferee if the transferee is an individual, or the identity and principal and local places of business of the transferee if the transferee is a corporation or other business entity:

Provided, That no other record keeping shall be required.

(d)(1) Any application submitted under subsection (a) or (b) of this section shall be approved if-

(A) the applicant is twenty-one years of age or over;

(B) the applicant (including, in the case of a corporation, partnership, or association, any individual possessing, directly or indirectly, the power to direct or cause the direction of the management and policies of the corporation, partnership, or association) is not prohibited from transporting, shipping, or receiving firearms or ammunition in interstate or foreign commerce under section 922(g) and (h) of this chapter;

(C) the applicant has not willfully violated any of the provisions of this chapter or regulations issued thereunder;

(D) the applicant has not willfully failed to disclose any material information required, or has not made any false statement as to any material fact, in connection with his application; and

(E) the applicant has in a State (i) premises from which he conducts business subject to license under this chapter or from which he intends to conduct such business within a reasonable period of time, or (ii) in the case of a collector, premises from which he conducts his collecting subject to license under this chapter or from which he intends to conduct such collecting within a reasonable period of time.

(2) The Secretary must approve or deny an application for a license within the forty-five-day period beginning on the date it is received. If the Secretary fails to act within such period, the applicant may file an action under section 1361 of title 28 to compel the Secretary to act. If the Secretary approves an applicant's application, such applicant shall be issued a license upon the payment of the prescribed fee.

(e) The Secretary may, after notice and opportunity for hearing, revoke any license issued under this section if the holder of such license has willfully violated any provision of this chapter or any rule or regulation prescribed by the Secretary under this chapter. The Secretary may, after notice and opportunity for hearing, revoke the license of a dealer who willfully transfers armor piercing ammunition. The Secretary's action under this subsection may be reviewed only as provided in subsection (f) of this section.

(f)(1) Any person whose application for a license is denied and any holder of a license which is revoked shall receive a written notice from the Secretary stating specifically the grounds upon which the application was denied or upon which the license was revoked. Any notice of a revocation of a license shall be given to the holder of such license before the effective date of the revocation.

(2) If the Secretary denies an application for, or revokes, a license, he shall, upon request by the aggrieved party, promptly hold a hearing to review his denial or revocation. In the case of a revocation of a license, the Secretary shall upon the request of the holder of the license stay the effective date of the revocation. A hearing held under this paragraph shall be held at a location convenient to the aggrieved party.

(3) If after a hearing held under paragraph (2) the

Secretary decides not to reverse his decision to deny an application or revoke a license, the Secretary shall give notice of his decision to the aggrieved party. The aggrieved party may at any time within sixty days after the date notice was given under this paragraph file a petition with the United States district court for the district in which he resides or has his principal place of business for de novo judicial review of such denial or revocation. In a proceeding conducted under this subsection, the court may consider any evidence submitted by the parties to the proceeding whether or not such evidence was considered at the hearing held under paragraph (2). If the court decides that the Secretary was not authorized to deny the application or to revoke the license, the court shall order the Secretary to take such action as may be necessary to comply with the judgment of the court.

(4) If criminal proceedings are instituted against a licensee alleging any violation of this chapter or of rules or regulations prescribed under this chapter, and the licensee is acquitted of such charges, or such proceedings are terminated, other than upon motion of the Government before trial upon such charges, the Secretary shall be absolutely barred from denying or revoking any license granted under this chapter where such denial or revocation is based in whole or in part on the facts which form the bases of such criminal charges. No proceedings for the revocation of a license shall be instituted by the Secretary more than one year after the filing of the indictment or information.

(g)(1)(A) Each licensed importer, licensed manufacturer, and licensed dealer shall maintain such records of importation, production, shipment, receipt, sale, or other disposition of firearms at his place of business for such period, and in such form as the Secretary may by regulations prescribe. Such importers, manufacturers, and dealers shall not be required to submit to the Secretary reports and information with respect to such records and the contents thereof, except as expressly required by this section. The Secretary, when he has reasonable cause to believe a violation of this chapter has occurred and that evidence thereof may be found on such premises, may, upon demonstrating such cause before a Federal magistrate and securing from such magistrate a warrant authorizing entry, enter during business hours the premises (including places of storage) of any licensed firearms importer, licensed manufacturer, licensed dealer, licensed collector, or any licensed importer or manufacturer of ammunition, for the purpose of inspecting or examining-

(i) any records or documents required to be kept by such licensed importer, licensed manufacturer, licensed dealer, or licensed collector under this chapter or rules or regulations under this chapter, and

(ii) any firearms or ammunition kept or stored by such licensed import, licensed manufacturer, licensed dealer, or licensed collector, at such premises.

(B) The Secretary may inspect or examine the inventory and records of a licensed importer, licensed manufacturer, or licensed dealer without such reasonable cause or warrant-

(i) in the course of a reasonable inquiry during the course of a criminal investigation of a person or persons other than the licensee;

(ii) for ensuring compliance with the record keeping requirements of this chapter not more than once during any twelve-month period; or

(iii) when such inspection or examination may be required for determining the disposition of one or more particular firearms in the course of a bona fide criminal investigation.

(C) The Secretary may inspect the inventory

and records of a licensed collector without such reasonable cause or warrant-

(i) for ensuring compliance with the record keeping requirements of this chapter not more than once during any twelve-month period; or

(ii) when such inspection or examination may be required for determining the disposition of one or more particular firearms in the course of a bona fide criminal investigation.

(D) At the election of a licensed collector, the annual inspection of records and inventory permitted under this paragraph shall be performed at the office of the Secretary designated for such inspections which is located in closest proximity to the premises where the inventory and records of such licensed collector are maintained. The inspection and examination authorized by this paragraph shall not be construed as authoring the Secretary to seize any records or other documents other than those records or documents constituting material evidence of a violation of law. If the Secretary seizes such records or documents, copies shall be provided the licensee within a reasonable time. The Secretary may make available to any Federal, State, or local law enforcement agency any information which he may obtain by reason of this chapter with respect to the identification of persons prohibited from purchasing or receiving firearms or ammunition who have purchased or received firearms or ammunition, together with a description of such firearms or ammunition, and he may provide information to the extent such information may be contained in the records required to be maintained by this chapter, when so requested by any Federal, State, or local law enforcement agency.

(2) Each licensed collector shall maintain in a

bound volume the nature of which the Secretary may by regulations prescribe, records of the receipt, sale, or other disposition of firearms. Such records shall include the name and address of any person to whom the collector sells or otherwise disposes of a firearm. Such collector shall not be required to submit to the Secretary reports and information with respect to such records and the contents thereof, except as expressly required by this section.

(3) Each licensee shall prepare a report of multiple sales or other dispositions whenever the licensee sells or otherwise disposes of, at one time or during any five consecutive business days, two or more pistols, or revolvers, or any combination of pistols and revolvers totalling two or more, to an unlicensed person. The report shall be prepared on a form specified by the Secretary and forwarded to the office specified thereon not later than the close of business on the day that the multiple sale or other disposition occurs.

(4) Where a firearms or ammunition business is discontinued and succeeded by a new licensee, the records required to be kept by this chapter shall appropriately reflect such facts and shall be delivered to the successor. Where discontinuance of the business is absolute, such records shall be delivered within thirty days after the business discontinuance to the Secretary. However, where State law or local ordinance requires the delivery of records to other responsible authority, the Secretary may arrange for the delivery of such records to such other responsible authority.

(5)(A) Each licensee shall, when required by letter issued by the Secretary, and until notified to the contrary in writing by the Secretary, submit on a form specified by the Secretary, for periods and at the times specified in such letter, all record information required to be kept by this chapter or such lesser record information as the Secretary in such letter may specify.

(B) The Secretary may authorize such record information to be submitted in a manner other than that prescribed in subparagraph (A) of this paragraph when it is shown by a licensee that an alternate method of reporting is reasonably necessary and will not unduly hinder the effective administration of this chapter. A licensee may use an alternate method of reporting if the licensee describes the proposed alternate method of reporting and the need therefor in a letter application submitted to the Secretary, and the Secretary approves such alternate method of reporting.

(h) Licenses issued under the provisions of subsection (c) of this section shall be kept posted and kept available for inspection on the premises covered by the license.

(i) Licensed importers and licensed manufacturers shall identify, by means of a serial number engraved or cast on the receiver or frame of the weapon, in such manner as the Secretary shall by regulations prescribe, each firearm imported or manufactured by such importer or manufacturer.

(j) A licensed importer, licensed manufacturer, or licensed dealer may, under rules or regulations prescribed by the Secretary, conduct business temporarily at a location other than the location specified on the license if such temporary location is the location for a gun show or event sponsored by any national, State, or local organization, or any affiliate of any such organization devoted to the collection, competitive use, or other sporting use of firearms in the community, and such location is in the State which is specified on the license. Records of receipt and disposition of firearms transactions conducted at such temporary location shall include the location of the sale or other disposition and shall be entered in the permanent records of the licensee and retained on the location specified on the license. Nothing in this subsection shall authorize any licensee to conduct business in or from any motorized or towed vehicle. Notwithstanding the provisions of subsection (a) of this section, a separate fee shall not be required of a licensee with respect to business conducted under this subsection. Any inspection or examination of inventory or records under this chapter by the Secretary at such temporary location shall be limited to inventory consisting of, or records relating to, firearms held or disposed at such temporary location. Nothing in this subsection shall be construed to authorize the Secretary to inspect or examine the inventory or records of a licensed importer, licensed manufacturer, or licensed dealer at any location other than the location specified on the license. Nothing in this subsection shall be construed to diminish in any manner any right to display, sell, or otherwise dispose of firearms or ammunition, which is in effect before the date of the enactment of the Firearms Owners' Protection Act.

(k) Licensed importers and licensed manufacturers shall mark all armor piercing projectiles and packages containing such projectiles for distribution in the manner prescribed by the Secretary by regulation. The Secretary shall furnish information to each dealer licensed under this chapter defining which projectiles are considered armor piercing ammunition as defined in section 921(a)(17)(B).

(Added Pub.L. 90-351, Title IV, 902, June 19, 1968, 82 State. 231, and amended Pub.L. 90-618, Title l, 102, Oct. 22, 1968, 82 State. 1221; Pub.L. 97-377, Title l, 165(b), Dec. 21, 1982, 96 Stat. 1923; Pub.L. 99-308, 103, May 19, 1986, 100 Stat. 453; Pub.L. 99-360, 1(c), July 8, 1986, 100 Stat. 766; Pub.L. 99-408, 3-7, Aug. 28, 1986, 100 Stat. 921.)

924. Penalties

(a)(1) Except as otherwise provided in paragraph (2) of this subsection, subsection (b) or (c) of this section, or in section 929, whoever-

(A) knowingly makes any false statement or representation with respect to the information required by this chapter to be kept in the records of a person licensed under this chapter or in applying for any license or exemption or relief from disability under the provisions of this chapter;

(B) knowingly violates subsection (a)(4), (a)(6), (f), (g), (i), (j), or (k) of section 922;

(C) knowingly imports or brings into the United States or any possession thereof any firearm or ammunition in violation of section 922(l); or

(D) willfully violates any other provision of this chapter,

shall be fined not more than $5,000, imprisoned not more than five years, or both, and shall become eligible for parole as the Parole Commission shall determine.

(2) Any licensed dealer, licensed importer, licensed manufacturer, or licensed collector who knowingly-

(A) makes any false statement or representation with respect to the information required by the provisions of this chapter to be kept in the records of a person licensed under this chapter, or

(B) violates subsection (m) of section 922,

shall be fined not more than $1,000, imprisoned not more than one year, or both, and shall become eligible for parole as the Parole Commission shall determine.

(b) Whoever with intent to commit therewith an offense punishable by imprisonment for a term exceeding one year, or with knowledge or reasonable cause to believe that an offense punishable by imprisonment for a term exceeding one year is to be committed therewith, ships, transports, or receives a firearm or any ammunition in interstate or foreign commerce shall be fined not more than $10,000, or imprisoned not more than ten years, or both.

(c)(1) Whoever, during and in relation to any crime of violence or drug trafficking crime, including a crime of violence or drug trafficking crime, which provides for any enhanced punishment if committed by the use of a deadly or dangerous weapon or device, for which he may be prosecuted in a court of the United States, uses or carries a firearm, shall, in addition to the punishment provided for such crime of violence or drug trafficking crime, be sentenced to imprisonment for five years, and if the firearm is a machinegun, or is equipped with a firearm silencer or firearm muffler, to imprisonment for ten years. In the case of his second or subsequent conviction under this subsection, such person shall be sentenced to imprisonment for ten years, and if the firearm is a machinegun, or is equipped with a firearm silencer or firearm muffler, to imprisonment for twenty years. Notwithstanding any other provision of law, the court shall not place on probation or suspend the sentence of any person convicted of a violation of this subsection, nor shall the term of imprisonment imposed under this subsection run concurrently with any other term of imprisonment including that imposed for the crime of violence or drug trafficking crime, or drug trafficking crime in which the firearm was used or carried. No person sentenced under this subsection shall be eligible for parole during the term of imprisonment imposed herein.

(2) For purposes of this subsection, the term "**drug trafficking crime**" means any felony violation of Federal law involving the distribution, manufacture, or importation of any controlled substance (as defined in section 102 of the Controlled Substances Act (21 U.S.C. 802)).

(3) For purposes of this subsection the term "**crime of violence**" means an offense that is a felony and-

(A) has as an element the use, attempted use, or threatened use of physical force against the person or property of another, or

(B) that by its nature, involves a substantial risk that physical force against the person or prop-

ertyof anothermaybe used in the course of committing the offense.

(d)(1) Any firearm or ammunition involved in or
used in any knowing violation of subsection (a)(4), (a)(6),
(f), (g), (h), (i), (j), or (k) of section 922, or knowing
importation or bringing into the United States or any
possession thereof any firearm or ammunition in violation
of section 922(l), or knowing violation of section 924, or
willful violation of any other provision of this chapter or
any rule or regulation promulgated thereunder, or any
violation of any other criminal law of the United States, or
any firearm or ammunition intended to be used in any
offense referred to in paragraph (3) of this subsection,
where such intent is demonstrated by clear and convincing
evidence, shall be subject to seizure and forfeiture, and all
provisions of the Internal Revenue Code of 1954 relating to
the seizure, forfeiture, and disposition of firearms, as
defined in section 5845(a) of that Code, shall, so far as
applicable, extend to seizures and forfeitures under the
provisions of this chapter:

Provided, That upon acquittal of the owner or
possessor, or dismissal of the charges against him other
than upon motion of the Government prior to trial, the
seized firearms or ammunition shall be returned forthwith
to the owner or possessor or to a person delegated by the
owner or possessor unless the return of the firearms or
ammunition would place the owner or possessor or his
delegate in violation of law. Any action or proceeding for
the forfeiture of firearms or ammunition shall be commenced within one hundred and twenty days of such
seizure.

(2)(A) In any action or proceeding for the return of
firearms or ammunition seized under the provisions of
this chapter, the court shall allow the prevailing party,
other than the United States, a reasonable attorney's fee,
and the United States shall be liable therefor.

(B) In any other action or proceeding under the provisions of this chapter, the court, when it finds that such action was without foundation, or was initiated vexatiously, frivolously, or in bad faith, shall allow the prevailing party, other than the United States, a reasonable attorney's fee, and United States shall be liable therefor.

(C) Only those firearms or quantities of ammunition particularly named and individually identified as involved in or used in any violation of the provisions of this chapter or any rule or regulation issued thereunder, or any other criminal law of the United States or as intended to be used in any offense referred to in paragraph (3) of this subsection, where such intent is demonstrated by clear and convincing evidence, shall be subject to seizure, forfeiture, and disposition.

(D) The United States shall be liable for attorney's fees under this paragraph only to the extent provided in advance by appropriation Acts.

(3) The offenses referred to in paragraphs (1) and (2)(C) of this subsection are-

(A) any crime of violence, as that term is defined in section 924(c)(3) of this title;

(B) any offense punishable under the Controlled Substances Act (21 U.S.C. 801 et seq.) or the Controlled Substances Import and Export Act (21 U.S.C. 951 et seq.);

(C) any offense described in section 922(a)(1), 922(a)(3), 922(a)(5), or 922(b)(3) of this title, where the firearm or ammunition intended to be used in any such offense is involved in a pattern of activities which includes a violation of any offense described in section 922(a)(1), 922(a)(3), 922(a)(5), 922(b)(3) of this title;

(e)(1) In the case of a person who violates section

922(g) of this title and has three previous convictions by any court referred to in section 922(g)(1) of this title for a violent felony or a serious drug offense, or both, such person shall be fined not more than $25,000 and imprisoned not less than fifteen years, and, notwithstanding any other provision of law, the court shall not suspend the sentence of, or grant a probationary sentence to, such person with respect to the conviction under section 922(g), and such person shall not be eligible for parole with respect to the sentence imposed under this subsection.

(2) As used in this subsection–

(A) the term **"serious drug offense"** means–

(i) an offense under the Controlled Substances Act (21 U.S.C. 801 et seq.), the Controlled Substances Import and Export Act (21 U.S.C. 951 et seq.), or the first section or section 3 of Public Law 96-350 (21 U.S.C. 955a et seq.), for which a maximum term of imprisonment of ten years or more is prescribed by law; or

(ii) an offense under State law, involving manufacturing, distributing, or possessing with intent to manufacture or distribute, a controlled substance (as defined in section 102 of the Controlled Substances Act (21 U.S.C. 802)), for which a maximum term of imprisonment of ten years or more is prescribed by law; and

(B) the term **"violent felon"** means any crime punishable by imprisonment for a term exceeding one year that–

(i) has as an element the use, attempted use, or threatened use of physical force against the person of another; or

(ii) is burglary, arson, or extortion, involves use of explosives, otherwise involves conduct that presents a serious potential risk of physical injury to another.

(Added Pub.L. 90-351, Title IV, 902, June 19, 1968, 82 Stat. 233, and amended Pub.L. 90-618, Title I, 102, Oct 22, 1968, 82 Stat. 1223; Pub.L. 91-644, Title II, 13, Jan. 2, 1971, 84 Stat. 1889; Pub.L. 98-473, Title II, 1005(a), Oct. 12, 1984, 98 Stat. 2138; Pub.L. 99-308, 104(a), May 19, 1986, 100 Stat. 456; Pub.L. 99-570, Title I, 1402, Oct. 27, 1986, 100 Stat. 3207.)

925. Exceptions: Relief from disabilities

(a)(1) The provisions of this chapter shall not apply with respect to the transportation, shipment, receipt, or importation of any firearm or ammunition imported for, sold or shipped to, or issued for the use of, the United States or any department or agency thereof or any State or any department, agency, or political subdivision thereof.

(2) The provisions of this chapter shall not apply with respect to

(A) the shipment or receipt of firearms or ammunition when sold or issued by the Secretary of the Army pursuant to section 4308 of title 10, and

(B) the transportation of any such firearm or ammunition carried out to enable a person, who lawfully received such firearm or ammunition from the Secretary of the Army, to engage in military training or in competitions.

(3) Unless otherwise prohibited by this chapter or any other Federal law, a licensed importer, licensed manufacturer, or licensed dealer may ship to a member of the United States Armed Forces on active duty outside the United States or to clubs, recognized by the Department of Defense, whose entire membership is composed of such members, and such members or clubs may receive a firearm or ammunition determined by the Secretary of the Treasury to be generally recognized as particularly suitable for sporting purposes and intended for the personal use of such member or club.

(4) was established to the satisfaction of the Secre-

tary to be consistent with the provisions of this chapter and other applicable Federal and State laws and published ordinances, the Secretary may authorize the transportation, shipment, receipt, or importation into the United States to the place of residence of any member of the United States Armed Forces who is on active duty outside the United States (or who has been on active duty outside the United States within the sixty day period immediately preceding the transportation, shipment, receipt, or importation), of any firearm or ammunition which is

   (A) determined by the Secretary to be generally recognized as particularly suitable for sporting purposes, or determined by the Department of Defense to be a type of firearm normally classified as a war souvenir, and

   (B) intended for the personal use of such member.

   (5) For the purpose of paragraphs (3) and (4) of this subsection, the term "United States" means each of the several States and the District of Columbia.

   (b) A licensed importer, licensed manufacturer, licensed dealer, or licensed collector who is indicted for a crime punishable by imprisonment for a term exceeding one year, may, notwithstanding any other provision of this chapter, continue operation pursuant to his existing license (if prior to the expiration of the term of the existing license timely application is made for a new license) during the term of such indictment and until any conviction pursuant to the indictment becomes final.

   (c) A person who is prohibited from possessing, shipping, transporting, or receiving firearms or ammunition may make application to the Secretary for relief from the disabilities imposed by Federal laws with respect to the acquisition, receipt, transfer, shipment, transportation, or possession of firearms, and the Secretary may grant such relief if it is established to his satisfaction that the circumstances regarding the conviction, and the applicant's record and reputation, are such that the applicant will not be likely to act in a manner dangerous to public safety and that the granting of the relief would not be contrary to the public interest. Any person whose application for relief from disabilities is denied by the Secretary may file a petition with the United states district court for the district in which he resides for a judicial review of such denial. The court may in its discretion admit additional evidence where failure to do so would result in a miscarriage of justice. A licensed importer, licensed manufacturer, licensed dealer, or licensed collector conducting operations under this chapter, who makes application for relief from the disabilities incurred under this chapter by reason of such a conviction, shall not be barred by such conviction from further operations under his license pending final action on an application for relief filed pursuant to this section. Whenever the Secretary grants relief to any person pursuant to this section he shall promptly publish in the FEDERAL REGISTER notice of such action, together with the reasons therefor.

(d) The Secretary shall authorize a firearm or ammunition to be imported or brought into the United States or any possession thereof if the firearm or ammunition-

(1) is being imported or brought in for scientific or research purposes, or is for use in connection with competition or training pursuant to chapter 401 of title 10;

(2) is an unserviceable firearm, other than a machinegun as defined in section 5845(b) of the Internal Revenue Code of 1954 (not readily restorable to firing condition), imported or brought in as a curio or museum piece;

(3) is of a type that does not fall within the definition of a firearm as defined in section 5845(a) of the Internal Revenue Code of 1954 and is generally recognized a particularly suitable for or readily adaptable to sporting

purposes, excluding surplus military firearms, except in any case where the Secretary has not authorized the importation of the firearm pursuant to this paragraph, it shall be unlawful to import any frame, receiver, or barrel of such firearm which would be prohibited if assembled; or

(4) was previously taken out of the United States or a possession by the person who is bringing in the firearm or ammunition.

The Secretary shall permit the conditional importation or bringing in of a firearm or ammunition for examination and testing in connection with the making of a determination as to whether the importation or bringing in of such firearm or ammunition will be allowed under this subsection.

(e) Notwithstanding any other provision of this title, the Secretary shall authorize the importation of, by any licensed importer, the following:

(1) All rifles and shotguns listed as curios or relics by the Secretary pursuant to section 921(a)(13), and

(2) All handguns, listed as curios or relics by the Secretary pursuant to section 921(a)(13), provided that such handguns are generally recognized a particularly suitable for or readily adaptable to sporing purposes.

(Added Pub.L. 90-351, Title IV, 902, June 19, 1968, 82 State. 233, and amended Pub.L. 90-618, Title I, 102, Oct. 22, 1968, 82 Stat. 1224; Pub.L. 98-573, Title II, 233, Oct. 30, 1984, 98 Stat. 2991; Pub.L. 99-308, 105, May 19, 1986. 100 Stat. 459.)

926. Rules and regulations

(a) The Secretary may prescribe only such rules and regulations as are necessary to carry out the provisions of this chapter, including-

(1) regulations providing that a person licensed under this chapter, when dealing with another person so licensed, shall provide such other licensed person a certified copy of this license; and

(2) regulations providing for the issuance, at a

reasonable cost, to a person licensed under this chapter, of certified copies of his license for use as provided under regulations issued under paragraph (1) of this subsection. No such rule or regulation prescribed after the date of the enactment of the Firearms Owner's Protection Act may require that records required to be maintained under this chapter or any portion of the contents of such records, be recorded at or transferred to a facility owned, managed, or controlled by the United States or any State or any political subdivision thereof, nor that any system of registration of firearms, firearms owners, firearms transactions or dispositions be established. Nothing in this section expands or restricts the Secretary's authority to inquire into the disposition of any firearm in the course of a criminal investigation.

(b) The Secretary shall give not less than ninety days public notice, and shall afford interested parties opportunity for hearing before prescribing such rules and regulations.

(c) The Secretary shall not prescribe rules or regulations that require purchasers of black powder under the exemption provided in section 845(a)(5) of this title to complete affidavits or forms attesting to that exemption.
(Added Pub.L. 90-351, Title IV, 902, June 19, 1968, 82 Stat. 234, and amended Pub.L. 90-618, Title I, 102 Oct. 22, 1968, 82 Stat. 1226; Pub.L. 99-308, 106, May 19, 1986, 100 Stat. 459.)

926A. Interstate transportation of firearms
Notwithstanding any other provision of any law or any rule or regulation of a State or any political subdivision thereof, any person who is not otherwise prohibited by this chapter from transporting, shipping, or receiving a firearm shall be entitled to transport a firearm for any lawful purpose from any place where he may lawfully possess and carry such firearm to any other place where he may lawfully possess and carry such firearm if, during such transportation the firearm is unloaded, and neither the firearm nor any ammunition being transported is

readily accessible or is directly accessible from the passenger compartment of such transporting vehicle:

Provided, That in the case of a vehicle without a compartment separate from the driver's compartment the firearm or ammunition shall be contained in a locked container other than the glove compartment or console.

(Added Pub.L. 99-360, 1(a), July 8, 1986, 100 Stat. 766.)

927. Effect on State law

No provision of this chapter shall be construed as indicating an intent on the part of the Congress to occupy the field in which such provision operates to the exclusion of the law of any State on the same subject matter, unless there is a direct and positive conflict between such provision and the law of the State so that the two cannot be reconciled or consistently stand together.

(Added Pub.L. 90-351, Title IV, 902, June 19, 1968, 82 Stat. 234, and amended Pub.L. 90-618, Title I, 102, Oct. 22, 1968, 82 Stat. 1226.)

928. Separability

If any provision of this chapter or the application thereof to any person or circumstance is held invalid, the remainder of the chapter and the application of such provision to other persons not similarly situated or to other circumstances shall not be affected thereby.

(Added Pub.L. 90-351, Title IV, 902, June 19, 1968, 82 Stat. 234, and amended Pub.L. 90-618, Title I, 102 Oct. 22, 1968, 82 Stat. 1226.)

929 Use of restricted ammunition

(a)(1) Whoever, during and in relation to the commission of a crime of violence or drug trafficking crime (including a crime of violence or drug trafficking crime which provides for an enhanced punishment if committed by the use of a deadly or dangerous weapon or device) for which he may be prosecuted in a court of the United States, uses or carries a firearm and is in possession of armor piercing ammunition capable of being fired in the firearm, shall, in addition to the punishment provided for the commission of such crime of violence or drug trafficking crime, be sentenced to a term of imprisonment for not less than five years.

(2) For purposes of this subsection, the term **"drug trafficking crime"** means any felony violations of Federal law involving the distribution, manufacture, or importation of any controlled substance (as defined in section 102 of the Controlled Substances Act (21 U.S.C. 802)).

(b) Notwithstanding any other provision of law, the court shall not suspend the sentence of any person convicted of a violation of this section, nor place the person on probation, nor shall the terms of imprisonment run concurrently with any other terms of imprisonment, including that imposed for the crime in which the armor piercing ammunition was used or possessed. No person sentenced under this section shall be eligible for parole during the term of imprisonment imposed herein.

(Added Pub.L. 98-473, Title II, 1006(a), oct. 12, 1984, 98 Stat. 2139; and amended Pub.L. 99-308, 108, May 19, 1986, 100 Stat. 460; Pub.L. 99-408, 8, Aug. 28, 100 Stat. 921.)

1968 Gun Control Act, Title II (Machine-guns and Destructive Devices ...)

Gun Control Act of 1968 (as Amended)

TITLE II-Machine Guns, Destructive Devices, and Certain Other Firearms
Title 26, U.S. Code Sections 5801-5872
SPECIAL (OCCUPATIONAL) TAXES

5801. Tax.

On first engaging in business and thereafter on or before the first day of July of each year, every importer, manufacturer, and dealer in firearms shall pay a special (occupational) tax for each place of business at the following rates:

(1) Importers. — $500 a year or fraction thereof;

(2) Manufacturers. — $500 a year or fraction thereof;

(3) Dealers. — $200 a year or fraction thereof;

Except an importer, manufacturer, or dealer who imports, manufactures, or deals in only weapons classified as "any other weapon" under section 5845(e), shall pay a special (occupational) tax for each place of business at the following rates: Importers, $25 a year or fraction thereof; manufacturers, $25 a year or fraction thereof; dealers, $10 a year or fraction thereof.

5802. Registration of importers, manufacturers, and dealers.

On first engaging in business and thereafter on or before the first day of July of each year, each importer, manufacturer, and dealer in firearms shall register with the Secretary in each internal revenue district in which such business is to be carried on, his name, including any trade name, and the address of each location in the district where he will conduct such business. Where there is a change during the taxable year in the location of, or the trade name used in, such business, the importer, manufacturer, or dealer shall file an application with the Secretary or his delegate to amend his registration. Firearms operations of an importer, manufacturer, or dealer may not be commenced at the new location or under a new trade name prior to approval by the Secretary or his delegate of the application.

TAX ON TRANSFERRING FIREARMS

5811. Transfer tax.

(a) Rate

There shall be levied, collected, and paid on firearms transferred a tax at the rate of $200 for each firearm transferred, except, the transfer tax on any firearm classified as any other weapon under section 5845(e) shall be at the rate of $5 for each such firearm transferred.

(b) By who paid

The tax imposed by subsection (a) of this section shall be paid by the transferor.

(c) Payment

The tax imposed by section (a) of this section shall be payable by the appropriate stamps prescribed for payment by the Secretary.

5812. Transfers.

(a) Application.

A firearm shall not be transferred unless (1) transferor of the firearm has filed with the Secretary a written application, in duplicate, for the transfer and registration of the firearm to the transferee on the application form prescribed by the Secretary; (2) any tax payable on the transfer is paid as evidenced by the proper stamp affixed to the original application form: (3) the transferee is identified in the application form in such manner as the Secretary may by regulations prescribe, except that, if such person is an individual, the identification must include his fingerprints and his photograph; (4) the transferor of the firearm is identified in the application form in such manner as the Secretary may by regulations prescribe; (5) the firearm is identified in the application form in such manner as the Secretary may by regulations prescribe; and (6) the application form shows that the Secretary has approved the transfer and the registration of the firearm to the transferee. Applications shall be denied if the transfer, receipt, or possession of the firearm would place the transferee in violation of law.

(b) Transfer of possession.

The transferee of a firearm shall not take possession of the firearm unless the Secretary has approved the transfer and registration of the firearm to the transferee as required by subsection (a) of this section.

TAX ON MAKING FIREARMS

5821. Making tax.

(a) Rate.

There shall be levied, collected, and paid upon the making of a firearm a tax at the rate of $200 for each firearm made.

(b) By whom paid.

The tax imposed by subsection (a) of this section

shall be paid by the person making the firearm.

(c) Payment.

The tax imposed by subsection (a) of this section shall be payable by the stamp prescribed for payment by the Secretary.

5822. Making.

No person shall make a firearm unless he has (a) filed with the Secretary a written application, in duplicate, to make and register the firearm on the form prescribed by the Secretary; (b) paid any tax payable on the making and such payment is evidenced by the proper stamp affixed to the original application form; (c) identified the firearm to be made in the application form in such manner as the Secretary may by regulations prescribe; (d) identified himself in the application form in such manner as the Secretary may by regulations prescribe, except that, if such person is an individual, the identification must include his fingerprints and his photograph; and (e) obtain the approval of the Secretary to make and register the firearm and the application form shows such approval. Applications shall be denied if the making or possession of the firearm would place the person making the firearm in violation of law.

5841. Registration of firearms.

(a) Central registry.

The Secretary shall maintain a central registry of all firearms in the United State which are not in the possession or under the control of the United States. This registry shall be known as the National Firearms Registration and Transfer Record. The registry shall include —

(1) identification of the firearm;

(2) date of registration; and

(3) identification and address of person entitled to possession of the firearm.

(b) By whom registered.

Each manufacturer, importer, and maker shall register each firearm he manufactures, imports, or makes. Each firearm transferred shall be registered to the transferee by the transferor.

(c) How registered.

Each manufacturer shall notify the Secretary of the manufacture of a firearm in such manner as may by regulations be prescribed and such notification shall effect the registration of the firearm required by this section. Each importer, make, and transferor of a firearm shall, prior to importing, making, or transferring a firearm, obtain authorization in such manner as required by this chapter or regulations issued thereunder to import, make, or transfer the firearm, and such authorization shall effect the registration of the firearm required by the section.

(d) Firearms registered on effective date of this act.

A person shown as possessing a firearm by the records maintained by the Secretary pursuant to the National Firearms Act in force on the day immediately prior to the effective date of the National Firearms Act of 1968 shall be considered to have registered under this section the firearms in his possession which are disclosed by that record as being in his possession.

(e) Proof of registration.

A person possessing a firearm registered as required by this section shall retain proof of registration which shall be made available to the Secretary upon request.

5842. Identification of firearms.

(a) Identification of firearms other than destructive devices.

Each manufacturer and importer and anyone making a firearm shall identify each firearm, other than a destructive device, manufactured, imported, or made by a serial number which may not be readily removed, obliterated, or altered, the name of the manufacturer, importer, or maker, and such other identification as the Secretary may by regulations prescribe.

(b) Firearms without serial number.

Any person who possesses a firearm, other than a destructive device, which does not bear the serial number and other information required by subsection (a) of this section shall identify the firearm with a serial number assigned by the Secretary and any other information the Secretary may by regulations prescribe.

(c) Identification of destructive device.

Any firearm classified as a destructive device shall be identified in such manner as the Secretary may by regulations prescribe.

5843. Records and returns.

Importers, manufacturers, and dealers shall keep records of, and render such returns in relation to, the importation, manufacture, making, receipt, and sale, or other disposition of firearms as the Secretary may by regulations prescribe.

5844. Importation.

No firearm shall be imported or brought into the United States or any territory under its control or jurisdiction unless the importer establishes, under regulations as may be prescribed by the Secretary, that the firearm to be imported or brought in is —

(1) being imported or brought in for the use of the United States or any department, independent establishment, or agency thereof or any State or possession or any political subdivision thereof; or

(2) being imported or brought in for scientific or research purposes; or

(3) being imported or brought in solely for testing

or use as a model by a registered manufacturer or solely for use as a sample by a registered importer or registered dealer;

except that, the Secretary may permit the conditional importation or bringing in of a firearm for examination and testing in connection with classifying the firearm.

5845. Definitions.

For the purpose of this chapter —
(a) Firearm.

The term "firearm" means (1) a shotgun having a barrel or barrels of less than 18 inches in length; (2) a weapon made from a shotgun if such weapon as modified has an overall length of less than 26 inches or a barrel or barrels of less than 18 inches in length; (3) a rifle having a barrel or barrels of less than 16 inches in length; (4) a weapon made from a rifle if such weapon as modified has an overall length of less than 26 inches or a barrel or barrels of less than 16 inches in length; (5) any other weapon, as defined in subsection (e); (6) a machine-gun; (7) a muffler or a silencer for any firearm whether or not such firearm is included within this definition; and (8) a destructive device. The term "firearm" shall not include an antique firearm or any device (other than a machine-gun or destructive device) which, although designed as a weapon, the Secretary finds by reason of the date of its manufacture, value, design, and other characteristics is primarily a collector's item and is not likely to be used as a weapon.
(b) Machine-gun.

The term "machine-gun" means any weapon which shoots, is designed to shoot, or can be readily restored to shoot, automatically more than one shot, without manual reloading, by a single function of the trigger. The term shall also include the frame or receiver of any such weapon, any combination of parts designed and intended for use in converting a weapon into a machine-gun, and any combination of parts from which a machine-gun can be assembled if such parts are in the possession or under the control of a person.

(c) Rifle.

The term "rifle" means a weapon designed or redesigned, made or remade, and intended to be fired from the shoulder and designed or redesigned and made or remade to use the energy of the explosive in a fixed cartridge to fire only a single projectile through a rifled bore for each single pull of the trigger, and shall include any such weapon which may be readily restored to fire a fixed cartridge.

(d) Shotgun.

The term "shotgun" means a weapon designed or redesigned, made or remade, and intended to be fired from the shoulder and designed or redesigned and made or remade to use the energy of the explosive in a fixed shotgun shell to fire through a smooth bore either a number of projectiles (ball shot) or a single projectile for each pull of the trigger, and shall include any such weapon which may be readily restored to fire a fixed shotgun shell.

(e) Any other weapon.

The term "any other weapon" means any weapon or device capable of being concealed on the person from which a shot can be discharged through the energy of an explosive, a pistol or revolver having a barrel with a smooth bore designed or redesigned to fire a fixed shotgun shell, weapons with combination shotgun and rifle barrels 12 inches or more, less than 18 inches in length, from which only a single discharge can be made from either barrel without manual reloading, and shall include any such weapon which may be readily restored to fire. Such terms shall not include a pistol or a revolver having a rifled bore, or rifled bores, or weapons designed, made, or intended to be fired from the shoulder and not capable of firing fixed ammunition.

(f) Destructive device.

The term "destructive device" means (1) any explosive, incendiary, or poison gas (A) bomb, (B) grenade, (C) rocket having propellant charge of more than four ounces, (D) missile having an explosive or incendiary charge of more than one-quarter ounce, (E) mine, or (F) similar device; (2) any type of weapon by whatever name known which will, or which may be readily converted to, expel a projectile by the action of an explosive or other propellant, the barrels of which have a bore of more than one-half inch in diameter, except a shotgun or shotgun shell which the Secretary finds is generally recognized as particularly suitable for sporting purposes; and (3) any combination of parts either designed or intended for use in converting any device into a destructive device as defined in subparagraphs (1) and (2) and from which a destructive device may be readily assembled. The term "destructive device" shall not include any device which is neither designed nor redesigned for use as a weapon; any device, although originally designed for use as a weapon, which is redesigned for use as a signaling, pyrotechnic, line throwing, safety or similar device; surplus ordnance sold, loaned, or given by the Secretary of the Army pursuant to the provisions of section 4684(2), 4685, or 4686 of title 10 of the United States Code; or any other device which the Secretary of the Treasury finds is not likely to be used as a weapon, or is an antique or is a rifle which the owner intends to use solely for sporting purposes.

(g) Antique firearm.

The term "antique firearm" means any firearm not designed or redesigned for using rim fire or conventional center fire ignition with fixed ammunition and manufactured in or before 1889 (including any matchlock, flintlock, percussion cap, or similar type of ignition system or replica thereof, whether actually manufactured before or after the year 1898) and also any firearm using fixed ammunition manufactured in or before 1898, for which ammunition is no longer manufactured in the United States and is not readily available in the ordinary channels of commercial trade.

(h) Unserviceable firearm.

The term "unserviceable firearm" means a firearm which is incapable of discharging a shot by means of an explosive and incapable of being readily restored to a firing condition.

(i) Make.

The term "make" and the various derivatives of such word, shall include manufacturing (other than by one qualified to engage in such business under this chapter), putting together, altering, and combination of these, or otherwise producing a firearm.

(j) Transfer.

The term "transfer" and the various derivatives of such word, shall include selling, assigning, pledging, leasing, loaning, giving away, or otherwise disposing of.

(k) Dealer.

The term "dealer" means any person, not a manufacturer or importer, engaged in the business of selling, renting, leasing, or loaning firearms and shall include pawnbrokers who accept firearms as collateral for loans.

(l) Importer.

The Term "importer" means any person who is engaged in the business of importing or bringing into the United States.

(m) Manufacturer.

The term "manufacturer" means any person who is engaged in the business of manufacturing firearms.

5846. Other laws applicable.

All provisions of law relating to special taxes imposed by chapter 51 and to engraving, issuance, sale, accountability, cancellation, and distribution of stamps for tax payment shall, insofar as not inconsistent with the provisions of this chapter, be applicable with respect to the taxes imposed by sections 5801, 5811, and 5821.

5847. Effect on other laws.
Nothing in this chapter shall be construed as modifying or affecting the requirements of section 414 of the Mutual Security Act of 1954, as amended, with respect to the manufacture, exportation, and importation of arms, ammunition, and implements of war.

5848. Restrictive use of information.
(a) General rule.
No information or evidence obtained from an application, registration, or records required to be submitted or retained by a natural person in order to comply with any provision of this chapter or regulations issued thereunder, shall, except as provided in subsection (b) of this section, be used, directly or indirectly, as evidence against that person in a criminal proceeding with respect to a violation of law occurring prior to or concurrently with the filing of the application or registration, or the compiling of the records containing the information or evidence.
(b) Furnishing false information.
Subsection (a) of this section shall not preclude the use of any such information or evidence in a prosecution or other action under any applicable provision of law with respect to the furnishing of false information.

5849. Citation of chapter.
This chapter may be cited as the "National Firearms Act" and any reference in any other provision of law to the "National Firearms Act" shall be held to refer to the provisions of this chapter.

5851. Special (occupational) tax exemption.
(a) Business with United States.

Any person required to pay special (occupational) tax under section 5801 shall be relieved from payment of tax if he establishes to the satisfaction of the Secretary that his business is conducted exclusively with, or on behalf of, the United States or any department, independent establishment, or agency thereof. The Secretary may relieve any person manufacturing firearms for, or on behalf of, the United States from compliance with any provision of this chapter in the conduct of such business.

(b) Application.

The exemption provided for in subsection (a) of this section may be obtained by filing with the Secretary an application on such form and containing such information as may by regulations be prescribed. The exemptions must thereafter be renewed on or before July 1 of each year. Approval of the application by the Secretary shall entitle the applicant to the exemption stated on the approved application.

5852. General transfer and making tax exemption.

(a) Transfer

Any firearm may be transferred to the United States or any department, independent establishment, or agency thereof, without payment of the transfer tax imposed by section 5811.

(b) Making by a person other than a qualified manufacturer.

Any firearm may be made by, or on behalf of, the Untied States, or any department, independent establishment, or agency thereof, without payment of the making tax imposed by section 5821.

(c) Making by a qualified manufacturer.

A manufacturer qualified under this chapter to engage in such business may make the type of firearm which he is qualified to manufacture without payment of the making tax imposed by section 5821.

(d) Transfers between special (occupational) taxpayers.

A firearm registered to a person qualified under this chapter to engage in business as an importer, manufacturer, or dealer may be transferred by that person without payment of the transfer tax imposed by section 5811 to any other person qualified under this chapter to manufacture, import, or deal in that type of firearm.

(e) Unserviceable firearm.

An unserviceable firearm may be transferred as a curio or ornament without payment of the transfer tax imposed by section 5811, under such requirements as the Secretary may by regulations prescribe.

(f) Right to exemption.

No firearm may be transferred or made exempt from tax under the provisions of this section unless the transfer or making is performed pursuant to an application in such form and manner as the Secretary may by regulations prescribe.

5853. Transfer and making tax exemption available to certain governmental entities.

(a) Transfer.

A firearm may be transferred without the payment of the transfer tax imposed by section 5811 to any State, possession of the United States, any political subdivision thereof, or any official police organization of such a government entity engaged in criminal investigations.

(b) Making.

A firearm may be made without payment of the making tax imposed by section 5821 by, or on behalf of, any State, or possession of the United States, any political subdivision thereof, or any official police organizations of such a government entity engaged in criminal investigations.

(c) Right to exemption.

No firearm may be transferred or made exempt

from tax under this section unless the transfer or making is performed pursuant to an application in such form and manner as the Secretary may by regulations prescribe.

5854. Exportation of firearms exempt from transfer tax.

A firearm may be exported without payment of the transfer tax imposed under section 5811 provided that proof of the exportation is furnished in such form and manner as the Secretary may by regulations prescribe.

5861. Prohibited acts.

It shall be unlawful for any person —

(a) to engage in business as a manufacturer or importer of, or dealer in, firearms without having paid the special (occupational) tax required by section 5801 for his business or having registered as required by section 5802; or

(b) to receive or possess a firearm transferred to him in violation of the provisions of this chapter;

(c) to receive or possess a firearm made in violation of the provisions of this chapter; or

(d) to receive or possess a firearm which is not registered to him in the National Firearms Registration and Transfer Record; or

(e) to transfer a firearm in violation of the provisions of this chapter; or

(f) to make a firearm in violation of the provisions of this chapter; or

(g) to obliterate, remove, change, or alter the serial number or other identification of a firearm required by this chapter; or

(h) to receive or possess a firearm having the serial number or other identification required by this chapter obliterated, removed, changed, or altered; or

(i) to receive or possess a firearm which is not identified by a serial number as required by the chapter; or

(j) to transport, deliver, or receive an firearm in interstate commerce which has not been registered as required by this chapter; or

(k) to receive or possess a firearm which has been imported or brought into the United States in violation of section 5844; or

(l) to make or cause the making of, a false entry on any application, return, or record required by this chapter, knowing such entry to be false.

5871. Penalties.

Any person who violates or fails to comply with any provision of this chapter shall, upon conviction, be fined not more than $10,000, or be imprisoned not more than ten years, or both, and shall become eligible for parole as the Board of Parole shall determine.

5872. Forfeitures.

(a) Laws applicable.

Any firearm involved in any violation of the provision of this chapter shall be subject to seizure and forfeiture, and (except as provided in subsection (b)) all the provisions of internal revenue laws relating to searches, seizures, and forfeitures of unstamped articles are extended to and made to apply to the articles taxed under this chapter, and the persons to whom this chapter applies.

(b) Disposal.

In the case of the forfeiture of any firearm by reason of a violation of this chapter, no notice of public sale shall be required; no such firearm shall be sold at public sale; if such firearm is forfeited for a violation of this chapter and there is no remission or mitigation of forfeiture thereof, it shall be delivered by the Secretary or his delegate to the Administrator of General Services, General Services Administration, who may order such firearm destroyed or may sell it to any State, or possession, or political subdivision thereof, or at the request of the Secretary, may authorize its retention for official use of the Treasury Department, or may transfer it without charge to any executive department or independent establishment of the Government for use by it.

Appenidix F

Federal Aviation Administration: Firearms Aboard Aircraft

Firearms Aboard Aircraft
Title 49, U.S. Code, Section 1472(L)
Note: This law, part of the Federal Aviation Act of 1958, as amended by the Air Transport Security Act of 1974, prohibits the carrying of any firearm, concealed or unconcealed, on or about the person or in carry-on baggage while aboard an air carrier. Unloaded firearms not accessible to the passenger while aboard the aircraft are permitted in compliance with FAA regulation 121.585(b), cited below.

The Federal Aviation Act is administered by the Federal Aviation Administration, U.S. Department of Transportation.

Section 1472 (L): Carrying Weapons or Explosives Aboard Aircraft
(1) Whoever, while aboard, or while attempting to board, any aircraft in, or intended for operation in, air transportation or intrastate air transportation, has on or about his person or his property a concealed deadly or dangerous weapon, which is, or would be, accessible to such person in flight, or any person who has on or about his person, or who has placed, attempted to place, or attempted to have placed aboard such aircraft any bomb, or similar explosive or incendiary device, shall be fined not more than $1,000 or imprisoned not more than one year, or both.

(2) Whoever willfully and without regard for the safety of human life, or with reckless disregard for the safety of human life, shall commit an act prohibited by paragraph (1) of this subsection, shall be fined not more than $5,000 or imprisoned not more than five years, or both.

(3) This subsection shall not apply to law enforcement officers of any municipal or State government, or the Federal Government, who are authorized or required within their official capacities to carry arms, or to persons who may be authorized, under regulations issued by the Administrator, to carry deadly or dangerous weapons in air transportation or intrastate air transportation; nor shall it apply to persons transporting weapons contained in baggage which is not accessible to passengers in flight if the presence of such weapons has been declared to the air carrier.

Under its general authority to "promote safety of flight of civil aircraft in air commerce" (49 USC * 1421(a)), the FAA has issued regulations which require persons traveling with firearms aboard common carrier aircraft to observe certain procedures. A violation is a misdemeanor punishable by a fine of up to $500 for the first offense and $2,000 thereafter.

Code of Federal Regulations, Title 14, Sec. 121.585(b):

(b) No certificate holder may knowingly permit any passenger to carry, nor may any passenger carry, while aboard an aircraft being operated by that certificate holder, in checked baggage, a deadly or dangerous weapon, unless the following conditions are met:

(1) The passenger has notified the certificate holder before checking the baggage that the weapon is in the baggage and that it is unloaded.

(2) The baggage in which the weapon is carried is locked, and only the passenger checking the baggage retains a key.

(3) The baggage is carried in an area other than the flight crew compartment that is inaccessible to passenger.

1968 Civil Rights Act

CIVIL RIGHTS ACT OF 1968. (P.L. 90-284)
TITLE X-Civil Disobedience Act of 1968
(Firearms in Civil Disorders)
Title 18, U.S. Code, Sections 231-233

231. Civil disorders.

(a) (1) Whoever teaches or demonstrates to any other person the use, application, or making of any firearm or explosive or incendiary device, or technique capable of causing injury or death to persons, knowing or having reason to know or intending that the same will be unlawfully employed for use in, or in furtherance of, a civil disorder which may in any way or degree obstruct, delay, or adversely affect commerce or the movement of any article or commodity in commerce or the conduct or performance of any federally protected functions; or

(2) Whoever transports or manufactures for transportation in commerce any firearm, or explosive or incendiary device, knowing or having reason to know or intending that the same will be used unlawfully in furtherance of a civil disorder; or

(3) Whoever commits or attempts to commit any act to obstruct, impeded, or interfere with any fireman or law enforcement officer lawfully engaged in the lawful performance of his official duties incident to and during

the commission of a civil disorder which in any way or degree obstructs, delays, or adversely affects commerce or the movement of any article or commodity in commerce or the conduct or performance of any federally protected function-

Shall be fined not more than $10,000 or imprisoned not more than five years, or both.

(b) Nothing contained in this section shall make unlawful any act of any law enforcement officer which is performed in the lawful performance of his official duties.

232. Definitions.

For the purposes of this chapter:

(1) The term "civil disorder" means any public disturbance involving acts of violence of assemblages of three or more persons, which causes an immediate danger of or results in damage or injury to the property or person of any other individual.

(2) The term "commerce" means commerce (A) between any State or the District of Columbia and any place outside thereof; (B) between points within any State or the District of Columbia, but through any place outside thereof; or (C) wholly within the District of Columbia.

(3) The term "federally protected function" means any function, operation, or action carried out, under the laws of the United States, by any department, agency, or instrumentality of the United States or by an officer or employee thereof; and such term shall specifically include, but not be limited to, the collection and distribution of the United States mails.

(4) The term "firearm" means any weapon which is designed to or may readily be converted to expel any projectile by the action of an explosive; or the frame or receiver of any such weapon.

(5) The Term "explosive or incendiary device" means (A) dynamite and all other forms of high explosives, (B) any explosive bomb, grenade, missile, or similar

device, and (C) any incendiary bomb or grenade, fire-bomb, or similar device, including any device which (i) consists of or includes a breakable container including a flammable liquid or compound, and a wick composed of any material which, when ignited, is capable of igniting such flammable liquid or compound, and (ii) can be carried or thrown by one individual acting alone.

(6) The term "fireman" means any member of a fire department (including a volunteer fire department) of any State, any political subdivision of a State, or the District of Columbia.

(7) The term "law enforcement officer" means any officer or employee of the United States, any State, any political subdivision of a State, or the District of Columbia, while engaged in the enforcement or prosecution of any of the criminal laws of the United States, a State, any political subdivision of a State, or the District of Columbia; and such term shall specifically include, but shall not be limited to, members of the National Guard, as defined in section 101(9) of title 10, United States Code, members of the organized militia of any State, or territory of the United States, the Commonwealth of Puerto Rico, or the District of Columbia, not included within the definition of National Guard as defined by such section 109(9), and members of the Armed Forces of the United States, while engaged in suppressing acts of violence or restoring law and order during a civil disorder.

233. Preemption.

Nothing contained in this chapter shall be construed as indicating an intent on the part of Congress to occupy the field in which any provisions of the chapter operate to the exclusion of State or local laws on the same subject matter, nor shall any provision of this chapter be construed to invalidate any provision of State law unless such provision is inconsistent with any of the purposes of this chapter or any provision thereof.

Appenidix H

Firearms in Federal Parks

USE AND POSSESSION OF FIREARMS IN NATIONAL PARKS

36 CFR 2.11

2.11 Firearms, traps, and other weapons.

(a) In natural and historical areas and national parkways, the use of a trap, seine, hand-thrown spear, net (except a landing net), firearm (including an air or gas powered pistol or rifle), blowgun, bow and arrow or crossbow, or any other implement designed to discharge missiles in the air or under the water which is capable of destroying animal life is prohibited. The possession of such object or implement is prohibited unless it is unloaded and cased or otherwise packed in such a way as to prevent its use while in the park areas.

(1) This paragraph (a) shall be applicable on the privately owned lands under the legislative jurisdiction of the United States within Glacier, Lassen Volcanic, Mesa Verde, Mount McKinley, Mount Rainier, Olympic, Rocky Mountain, Sequoia-Kings Canyon, Yellowstone, and Yosemite National Parks.

(2) When authorized by the superintendent, licensed guides in charge of pack trains or saddle horse parties may carry firearms for emergency use as stipulated in a written permit.

(3) Authorized federal, state, county, and city law enforce-

ment officers may carry firearms in the performance of their official duties.

(b) In recreational areas (except national parkways) the use and possession of all firearms or other implements designed to discharge missiles, which are capable of destroying animal life, shall conform with all applicable, federal, state, and local laws. Such firearms or other implements shall not be used in a manner so as to endanger person or property. The possession of loaded firearms or other implements in developed, populated, or concentrated use areas is prohibited.

Appenidix I

Exportation and Importation of Firearms

Exportation-regualtions 22 CFR 121-128 (International Traffic in Arms Regulations) under the authority of the Mutual Security Act of 1954, Executive Orders' 11432 and 10973, as superseded by the Arms Control Act of 1976.

Exportation

All manufacturers and exporters of firearms must register with the Office of Munitions Control of the U.S. Department of State which maintains the U.S. Munitions List for the purpose of restricting the flow of arms abroad. The list includes, among other weapons, all firearms up to and including .50 caliber except shotguns with barrels 18 inches long and over. Export permits are required by the Office of Munitions Control for the exportation of any items on the Munitions List except pre-1898 firearms on presentation of sufficient authentication of age.

Also, an individual is permitted to export three nonautomatic firearms and 1,000 cartridges for such firearms for that person's personal use when the firearms are with the person's baggage or effects whether accompanied or unaccompanied (but not mailed). Special exemptions are provided for members of the Armed Forces and civilian employees of the U.S. government.

Minor components of items on the Munitions List may be exported without a permit if the total transaction does not exceed $100 in value.

Licensed manufacturers, licensed importers, and licensed dealers exporting firearms and ammunition are required to maintain records showing which firearms and ammunition were exported, to which foreign consignees the firearms or ammunition were sent, and on which date they were exported.

Importation

The Gun Control Act of 1968 controls all firearms and ammunition importation except the importation of airguns, antiques, and replicas of antiques. Title 1 weapons (handguns, rifles, and shotguns) may be imported by a holder of a Federal Firearms License. If a dealer wishes to make importations on a regular basis, the dealer would be considered to be "engaging in the business" of importing and would require a special importer's license which may be obtained from the Bureau of Alcohol, Tobacco and Firearms. Title II firearms (machineguns, other fully automatic firearms, destructive devices, etc.) and military surplus firearms may not be imported except for use in research, for scientific use, or for government use. However military surplus ammunition suitable for sporting purposes may be imported. Title II importations are handled by the director of the BATF on a case-by-case basis.

Permits must be obtained from the BATF for the importation of items on the Munitions List which are not covered by the Gun Control Act of 1968. Although antique firearms are specifically excluded from any import restrictions, replicas are not and importers of black-powder firearms made in 1898 or after must secure a BATF import permit.

Appenidix J

Postal Regulations on the Mailing of Firearms

124.4 FIREARMS, KNIVES AND SHARP INSTRUMENTS (18 U.S.C. 1715, 1716)

.41 Pistols, Revolvers and Other Concealable Firearms
.411 General

Pistols, revolvers and other firearms capable of being concealed on the person (hereinafter referred to as hand guns) are nonmailable except when mailed between the parties specified in 124.413 and 124.415 and upon the filing of an affidavit or statement as required by 124.414 and 124.416.

.412 Definitions

(a) The term "hand gun" means any pistol, revolver or other firearm or device the mailing of which is regulated by this section,

(b) The term "pistol" or "revolver" means a hand gun styled to be fired by the use of a single hand and to fire or otherwise expel a projectile by the action of an explosive, spring, or other mechanical action, or air- or gas-pressure with sufficient force to be used as a weapon.

(c) The term "firearm" means any device, including a starter gun, which is designed to or may readily be converted to expel a projectile by the action of an explosion, spring, or other mechanical action, or air- or gas pressure with sufficient force to be used as a weapon.

(d) The phrase "other firearms capable of being concealed on the person" includes, but is not limited to, short-barreled shotguns, and short-barreled rifles.

(e) The term "short-barreled shotgun" means a shotgun having one or more barrels less than 18 inches in length. The term "short-barreled rifle" means a rifle having one or more barrels less than 16 inches in length. These definitions include any weapon made from a shotgun or rifle, whether by alteration, modification or otherwise, if such weapon as modified has an overall length of less than 26 inches. A short-barreled shotgun or rifle of greater dimension may also be regarded as nonmailable when it has characteristics allowing it to be concealed on the person.

(f) The terms "licensed manufacturer" and "licensed dealer" mean, respectively, a manufacturer of firearms or a bona-fide dealer therein, duly licensed by the Bureau of Alcohol, Tobacco and Firearms of the Department of the Treasury, pursuant to the Gun Control Act of 1968 (Public Law 90-618), 18 U.S.C. 921, et seq.

(g) The term "antique firearm" means any firearm (including those with a matchlock, flintlock, percussion cap, or similar type of ignition system) manufactured in or before 1898, or any replica thereof if such replica-

(1) is not designed or redesigned for using rimfire or conventional centerfire fixed ammunition, or

(2) uses rimfire or conventional centerfire fixed ammunition, which is no longer manufactured in the United States and which is not readily available in the ordinary channels of commercial trade.

.413 Mailings Between Authorized Persons

Subject to the requirements of 124.414, hand guns may be mailed by a licensed manufacturer of firearms, a licensed dealer therein, or an authorized agent of the Federal Government or the government of a State, District or Territory, only when addressed to a person in one of the following categories for use in connection with his official duties:

(a) officers of the Army, Navy, Air Force, Coast Guard, Marine Corps, or Organized Reserve Corps;

(b) officers of the National Guard or Militia of a State, Territory or District whose official duty is to serve warrants of arrest or commitment;

(c) officers of the United States or of a State, Territory or District whose official duty is to serve warrants of arrest or commitment;

(d) employees of the Postal Service specifically authorized by the Chief Postal Inspector;

(e) officers and employees of enforcement agencies of the United States;

(f) watchmen engaged in guarding the property of the United States, a State, Territory or District;

(g) purchasing agent or other designated member of agencies employing officers and employees included in c, d, and e.

.414 Affidavit of Addressee Required

Any person proposing to mail a hand gun pursuant to 124.413 must file with the postmaster, at the time of mailing, an affidavit signed by the addressee setting forth that he is qualified to receive the firearm under the particular category (a) through (g) of 124.413, and that the firearm is intended for his official use. The affidavit must also bear a certificate stating that the firearm is for the official duty use of the addressee, signed by one of the following as appropriate:

(a) for officers of Armed Forces, a certificate by the commanding officer;:

(b) for officers and employees of enforcement agencies, a certificate signed by the head of the agency employing the addressee to perform the official duty in connection with which the firearm is to be used:

(c) for watchmen, a certificate signed by the chief clerk of the department, bureau or independent branch of the Government of the United States, the State, the Territory, or the District by which the watchman is employed:

(d) for the purchasing agent or other designated member of enforcement agencies, a certificate signed by the head of such agency, that the firearm is to be used by an officer or employee included in (c), (d), and (e) of 124.413.

.415 Mailings Between Licensed Manufacturers and Dealers

Hand guns may also be conveyed in the mails between licensed manufacturers of firearms and licensed dealers therein in customary trade shipments, or for repairs or replacement of parts.

.416 Certificate of Manufacturers and Dealers

A licensed manufacturer or dealer need not file the affidavit required under 124.414, but must file with the postmaster a statement (Form 1508, "Statement by Shipper of Firearms") signed by the mailer that he is a licensed manufacturer of firearms or dealer therein, that the parcels containing handguns (or major component parts thereof) are customary trade shipments or contain such articles for repair or replacement of parts, and that to the best of his knowledge or belief the addressees are licensed manufacturers of firearms or dealers therein. If satisfied with the mailer's statement, the postmaster will accept the parcels for mailing. If the postmaster is not satisfied with the mailer's statement, he will forward it to the Director, Office of Mail Classification, Rates and Classification Department, for a ruling.

.417 Federal Bureau of Investigation; Crime Detection Bureaus

Hand guns addressed to the Federal Bureau of Investigation, or its Director, or to the scientific laboratory or crime detection bureau of any agency whose members are federal law-enforcement officers or officers of a State, Territory, or District authorized to serve warrants or arrest or commitment, may be accepted for mailing without regard to the provisions of 124.413 through 124.416.

.418 Official Shipments

Hand guns may be accepted for mailing, without regard to the provisions of 124.413 through 124.416, when offered by an authorized agent of the Federal Government as an official shipment to any qualified addressee in categories (a) through (g) of 124.413, or to a licensed manufacturer of firearms or dealer therein or to a Federal agency.

.42 Antique Firearms

Antique firearms sent as curios or museum pieces may be accepted for mailing without regard to the provisions of 124.413 through 124.416.

.43 Rifles and Shotguns

While unloaded rifles and shotguns not precluded by 124.411 and 124.412(e) are mailable, mailers are responsible for compliance with the Gun Control Act of 1968, Public Law 90-618, 18 U.S.C. 921, et seq., and the rules and regulations promulgated thereunder, 26 CFR 178, as well as State and local laws. The mailer may be required by the Postal Service to establish, by opening of the parcel or by written certification, that the gun is unloaded and not precluded by 124.412(e). It is recommended that all such mailings be sent by registered mail.

.44 legal Opinions About Mailing Firearms

Postmasters are not authorized to give opinions concerning the legality of any shipment of rifles or shotguns (see 123.34).

.46 Marking of Parcels of Firearms and Switchblade Knives

No marking of any kind which would indicate the nature of the contents shall be placed on the outside wrapper or container of any parcel containing firearms or switchblade knives.

Appenidix K

1968 Omnibus Crime Control and Safe Streets Act

OMNIBUS CRIME CONTROL AND SAFE STREETS ACT OF 1968 (P.L. 90-351)
TITLE VII-Unlawful Possession or Receipt of Firearms
Title 18 U.S. Code-Appendix, Sections 1201-1203

1201. Congressional findings and declaration.
The Congress hereby finds and declares that the receipt, possession, or transportation of a firearm by felons, veterans who are discharged under dishonorable conditions, mental incompetents, aliens who are illegally in the country, and former citizens who have renounced their citizenship, constitutes-
(1) a burden on commerce or threat affecting the free flow of commerce,
(2) a threat to the safety of the President of the United States and Vice President of the United States,
(3) an impediment or a threat to the exercise of free speech and the free exercise of a religion guaranteed by the first amendment to the Constitution of the United States, and
(4) a threat top the continued and effective operation of the Government of the United States and of the government of each State guaranteed by article IV of the Constitution.

1202. Receipt, possession, or transportation of firearms.
(a) Persons liable; penalties for violations.

Any person who—
(1) has been convicted by a court of the United States or of a State or any political subdivision thereof of a felony, or
(2) has been discharged from the Armed Forces under dishonorable conditions, or
(3) has been adjudged by a court of the United States or of a State or any political subdivision thereof of being mentally incompetent, or
(4) having been a citizen of the United States has renounced his citizenship, or
(5) being an alien is illegally or unlawfully in the United States,

and who receives, possesses, or transports in commerce or affecting commerce, after the date of enactment of this act, any firearm shall be fined not more than $10,000 or imprisoned for not more than two years, or both.

(b) Employment; persons liable; penalties for violations.

Any individual who to his knowledge and while being employed by any persons who—
(1) has been convicted by a court of the United States or of a State or any political subdivision thereof of a felony, or
(2) has been discharged from the Armed Forces under dishonorable conditions, or
(3) has been adjudged by a court of the United States or of a State or any political subdivision thereof of being mentally incompetent, or
(4) having been a citizen of the United States has renounced his citizenship, or
(5) being an alien is illegally or unlawfully in the United States,

and who, in the course of such employment, receives, possesses, or transports in commerce or affecting commerce, after the date of the enactment of this Act, any firearm shall be fined not more than $10,000 or imprisoned for not more than two years, or both.

(c) Definitions.

As used in this title-

(1) "commerce" means travel, trade, traffic, commerce, transportation, or communication among the several States, or between the District of Columbia and any State, or between any foreign country or any territory or possession and any State or the District of Columbia, or between points in the same State but through any other State or the District of Columbia or a foreign country:

(2) "felony" means any offense punishable by imprisonment for a term exceeding one year, but does not include any offense (other than one involving a firearm or explosive) classified as a misdemeanor under the laws of a State and punishable by a term of imprisonment of two years or less;

(3) "firearms" means any weapon (including a starter gun) which will or is designed to or may readily be converted to expel a projectile by the action of an explosive; the frame or receiver of any such weapon; or any firearm muffler or firearm silencer; or any destructive device. Such term shall include any handgun, rifle, or shotgun;

(4) "destructive device" means any explosive, incendiary, or poison gas bomb, grenade, mine, rocket, missile, or similar device; and includes any type of weapon which will or is designed to or may readily be converted to expel a projectile by the action of any explosive and having a barrel with a bore of one-half inch or more in diameter;

(5) "handgun" means any pistol or revolver originally designed to be fired by the use of a single hand and which is designed to fire or capable of firing fixed cartridge ammunition, or any other firearm originally designed to be fired by the use of a single hand;

(6) "shotgun" means a weapon designed or redesigned, made or remade, and intended to be fired from the shoulder and designed or redesigned and made or remade to use the energy of the explosive in a fixed shotgun shell to

fire through a smooth bore either a number of ball shot or a single projectile for each single pull of the trigger;

(7) "rifle" means a weapon designed or redesigned, made or remade, and intended to be fired from the shoulder and designed or redesigned and made or remade to use the energy of the explosive in a fixed metallic cartridge to fire only a single projectile through a rifled bore for each single pull of the trigger.

1203. Exemptions.

This title shall not apply to-

(1) any person who by reason of duties connected with law enforcement has expressly been entrusted with a firearm by competent authority of the prison; and

(2) any person who has been pardoned by the President of the United States or the chief executive of a State and has expressly been authorized by the President or such chief executive, as the case may be, to receive, possess, or transport in commerce a firearm.